PENGUIN BOOKS

MY JOURNEY WITH THE ANGELS

My Journey with
the Angels

PATRICIA BUCKLEY

PENGUIN BOOKS

PENGUIN BOOKS

Published by the Penguin Group
Penguin Books Ltd, 80 Strand, London WC2R ORL, England
Penguin Group (USA) Inc., 375 Hudson Street, New York, New York 10014, USA
Penguin Group (Canada), 90 Eglinton Avenue East, Suite 700, Toronto, Ontario, Canada M4P 2Y3
(a division of Pearson Penguin Canada Inc.)
Penguin Ireland, 25 St Stephen's Green, Dublin 2, Ireland (a division of Penguin Books Ltd)
Penguin Group (Australia), 250 Camberwell Road,
Camberwell, Victoria 3124, Australia (a division of Pearson Australia Group Pty Ltd)
Penguin Books India Pvt Ltd, 11 Community Centre,
Panchsheel Park, New Delhi – 110 017, India
Penguin Group (NZ), 67 Apollo Drive, Rosedale, Auckland 0632, New Zealand
(a division of Pearson New Zealand Ltd)
Penguin Books (South Africa) (Pty) Ltd, 24 Sturdee Avenue,
Rosebank, Johannesburg 2196, South Africa

Penguin Books Ltd, Registered Offices: 80 Strand, London WC2R ORL, England

www.penguin.com

First published by Penguin Ireland 2011
Published in Penguin Books 2011
004

Set in 12.02/14.23pt Garamond MT
Typeset by Jouve (UK), Milton Keynes
Printed in England by Clays Ltd, St Ives plc

ISBN: 978-0-141-04915-1

www.greenpenguin.co.uk

ALWAYS LEARNING   PEARSON

This book is dedicated to the memory of my dear brother John, who went home to the angels on 25 January 2009.

You will be forever a guiding light.

Also to my faithful friend and companion, our little Yorkshire terrier Dutcho, who blessed our lives for nearly fourteen years. She flew home to the angels on 20 May 2010.

Contents

CONTENTS

Prologue

The angels are always showing me, in different ways, that they are with me. They never cease to amaze me. I have so many stories, but my favourite happened in our angel shop, some years ago.

I was there by myself, on a miserable wet morning, and the shop was really quiet. A petite woman in her twenties came into the shop. She was beautiful, with blonde hair and a tiny oval-shaped face. She looked at me with these huge blue eyes. I couldn't help but look at her. She had a bright light all around her and a very calming energy.

'Do you have a pen and paper I could borrow?' she asked.

Still looking at her, and in awe of her energy, I got her the pen and paper, and I pulled up a chair for her too, so that she could write in comfort. She sat in the corner of the shop, and she was writing away so much that she didn't look up. Not once. I couldn't help but smile as I watched her. The light around her grew brighter and brighter. I remember thinking, *She looks like an angel*. Then she stood up, walked to the desk and put the piece of paper down.

'This is for you.'

'Thank you.' I still couldn't take my eyes off her.

'Always remember to follow your dreams.' I smiled. 'And something I must tell you. Your angels are very happy that you are back.'

'How do you know all this?' I was amazed. Then she gave

me a smile. It was a smile I had seen many times when I was a little girl. It was the very same smile that the angels give me.

'I've something else for you.' She rummaged in a bag and handed me two little angels standing on a rainbow. There was a candle too. Then she gave me a crystal stone that has a rainbow in it.

I was so surprised that no words came. Then she picked the paper up from the desk and handed it to me. As I took it I felt a kind of electric shock like a warm flow of energy running through me.

She looked at me with those piercing blue eyes and smiled that amazing smile.

'Keep on your path,' she said. 'There are many more angels with you.' Then she left.

I opened the paper and saw that she had written the words to the song 'Somewhere over the Rainbow'.

That song from *The Wizard of Oz* has always been my very favourite song. I loved it when I was a child, and I still love it today because it is all about dreaming and believing.

I have never seen her again, but I remember her every day. I still have the two angels and the crystal that she gave me that day. I keep them by my bed. Every time I look at them I see that beautiful angel lady who graced me with her presence that day.

1 A Hard Start

Every day, I ask my angel for healing
around the world.

When I was six years old, I saw a boy who had drowned. He was in a small back bedroom in my mam's parents' house in Crumlin. It was days before my first holy communion. I'd run into the room to collect my dress. I was so excited! And there, between the iron fireplace and an old cot, was this little boy. He turned when he saw me, and smiled.

'Hello, Patricia.'

I jumped back and just stared at him. I'd never seen him before in my life, and I couldn't imagine what he was doing there.

'How do you know my name?'

He didn't answer. He just looked at me with those huge brown eyes. I thought he was strange. He was wearing funny clothes. He had on grey flannel shorts and a blazer. Like a school uniform from the olden days. We stood, looking at each other in that cold, damp room. Then I heard Mam shouting my name, so I left him there. I ran downstairs with my dress.

'Oh, there you are,' said Mam. 'What took look you so long?'

'I was talking to the boy.'

'What boy?'

'The boy that was in the room.'

She looked at me strangely then.

'Oh yes? And what did he look like, this boy?'

I shrugged. 'He was just a boy.' I paused. 'But his clothes were all wet.' That was something that had puzzled me. There was no water around, yet he'd been dripping wet.

I still find that very strange. And at that time I was really confused. As for Mam, she just shouted at me.

She looked white with shock, yet she was angry. 'Girls who lie,' she said, 'can't make their communion.' I couldn't think what I'd done wrong. Years later I understood. Mam told me he'd been a childhood friend of hers. He'd gone to school with her, but had drowned, climbing into some kind of tank.

That day, though, I was upset by her shouting. I started to cry. Why couldn't she believe me?

Since that time, I've had regular encounters with the spirit world. I can see them, feel them and communicate with them as easily as I can with the living. Sometimes more easily. I have a spirit guide that helps me in my work, passing on messages from those who have left this life to their loved ones. Through this I have learned many things about what awaits us after we die.

I now see this as a blessing. I have no fear of death, having seen the other side. But for much of my life it's been a burden. It's hurt me because others would not accept what I could see. And that included my family. It almost cost me my sanity, and my life.

I had always been aware of angels. They were just there. At first I was just aware of lights and a good, warm feeling. But I always somehow knew that angels were there. Later on they became definite beings; beings who talked to me and protected me. The angels who appear to me now are beings of such astonishing light and beauty that sometimes I feel overcome when they appear. They have been with me all my life, although there were years when I denied their existence. Yet their incredible presence can still make me giddy.

I was born in Dublin in 1961. Or possibly in 1960. There was always a lot of confusion.

My mam was living with her mam, my Nanny Chris, at the time, in Clonard Road in Crumlin. She was twenty, or maybe still nineteen. And one day, they went for a walk over to my great-aunt Katie's house in Rafter's Road. Aunt Katie had a massive amount of kids. But she was a great mam. She was always very good to them.

It was such a funny house. The door was always open. There was always laughter there, and always lots of people. There'd be two kettles on the hob, constantly going, and she'd have a big pot of soup too. She'd offer it to everyone who came in. She loved her children, and dedicated everything to their upbringing. She had ten of them. Her eldest was Mam's age, and her youngest was five when I was born.

While they were there, drinking tea in the kitchen, Mam started to have contractions. And she went a bit strange. I'm not sure if she realized that she *was* in labour. All she knew for certain was that she was in this terrible pain. I think it scared her. And she didn't want anyone around while she dealt with it. So she locked herself into the toilet and wouldn't let anybody in. There was chaos! Everybody was running around in a panic. Nobody knew what to do. Eventually Aunt Katie managed to coax Mam out of the toilet, but by then I was half born. My head was already out.

Mam *still* didn't realize. I suppose she was just in a state. She thought she was going to the toilet, and she wasn't listening to anyone. At that point, my dad came up the stairs. At the sight of him Mam freaked and went back into the toilet. She locked it again. She didn't want anybody to see her. And I was born down the toilet. It wasn't a great start – I still get slagged over it even now.

Katie went in, calmed Mam down, and sorted her out. She always was the practical one. Eventually the midwife arrived and cut my cord.

My dad was in the Irish army at the time. Mam was working in Swan Dry Cleaners in Crumlin when they met at a dance. Dad was a charmer. He was small and dapper, with dark hair he kept neatly combed. I can see why Mam liked him. It was easy to see why he liked her too. She was a striking woman back then. Small and petite, she had this amazing hair. It was jet black, thick, and very, very long. She was very pretty. She has these deep, deep blue eyes. Her dad used to sing 'Nancy with the Smiling Eye' to her. I always remember that.

Soon after Mam and Dad met, Dad was sent away with the army. They kept in touch until he came back, and in the end they went off to England together and came back married. Mam's mam, Nanny Chris, wasn't one bit pleased. She didn't approve of my dad. He was too different from her husband, Granddad Tommy. He was reliable and very hard-working, and maybe she sensed that Dad was not.

Dad went to the Congo soon after I was born. And then, when he got back, Mam, Dad and myself moved over to England. Mam was pregnant again, and my sister Liz was born in England when I was two years old. We moved back to Ireland briefly, and stayed with Nanny Chris, but by the time Mam was pregnant for the third time, we were living in England again.

This was because Dad had got kicked out of the Irish army. Knowing Dad, that wasn't so surprising. He didn't take too well to discipline. He was kicked out for fighting and drinking, and for general bad behaviour. That's Dad for you. But what did he do when he got kicked out? He joined the English army.

The thing was, though, he didn't change. I don't think he was capable of it. So he didn't last long there either. By the time Mam was due to have her third baby, Dad was trying to get Mam, myself and my sister back to Ireland, and he went AWOL. I don't remember it, but they've told me we were on our way back to Ireland when Mam went into labour. This time she knew what was happening. They didn't get on the boat, and my brother John ended up being born in Romford in Essex.

Meanwhile the military police were out looking for Dad. He was caught in the end, and was sentenced. He was sent to prison in Romford.

Mam never talked much about that time. Dad has always told me Mam didn't like it there. She had to stay in military quarters and she found that hard with Dad in prison. She had nothing in common with the other women, and she found it hard to make friends with them. She missed her family too. She hated being away from them. It didn't seem right to her. So when Dad was released and discharged, we all came back to Ireland again. And pretty soon, Mam became pregnant yet again.

After we moved back that time, we lived in a flat in Foley Street. It's in Dublin's north inner city. I can remember it there clearly. It was *not* a happy home. There was never any money, and the electricity was always being turned off. It could be freezing in that flat.

And then there was my dad. He'd left the army, but he hadn't changed his ways. He was still a drinker. Nothing could change that. And he could be violent – mostly to Mam, but to us children too. And that wore my mam down.

We were living there when I was six, and when I saw that drowned boy. I made my first holy communion from that flat; because, of course, there was never really any question about that. The only question was, which dress would I wear? I was the first grandchild on Mam's side, and only the third on Dad's. All my grandparents were so proud of me. So proud that both sets had bought me dresses. I ended up with two dresses and two coats. That was so exciting – especially when I never normally had anything new.

It was really funny, though at the time, I remember there was a bit of disagreement about it. It's like my two nannies were jealous of each other. Nanny Chris was half Italian. She loved clothes, and she could be quite stubborn. She decided because I was her first grandchild that she would buy my outfit. She took me to Thomas Street and bought the whole outfit. That included a beautiful salmon-pink coat. It had these lovely big buttons.

The next time I saw Nanny Bridget, I told her about my outfit. I was so excited, because I wasn't used to having new clothes. I thought she'd be pleased for me, but she didn't look that happy.

'Is that right?' She then took me into town, into the posh area around Grafton Street, and bought me another dress. She bought me a coat too. It was mint green.

Dad said I should wear the outfit his mam had bought, but Nanny Chris could be really stubborn.

Anyway, in the end there was a compromise. I wore Nanny Chris's dress on my communion day, but with the green coat

Nanny Bridget had given me. And the next day, when I went back to the church, I wore the pink coat and Nanny Bridget's dress.

I remember getting ready for my communion. Nanny Chris was helping me get my hair right, and my veil straight. I felt like a princess. The church was near St Theresa's Gardens. When we arrived there, on the day of my communion, we were all wild with excitement. My school friends and I were comparing our outfits. We were spinning around to show the full skirts off. But after we'd taken our places at the front of the church – divided boy, girl, boy, girl – I noticed there was an empty chair where one of the girls should have been.

The girl who wasn't there was a friend of mine; someone I often used to play with in the playground. I remember thinking, *Oh, she's not here yet.* I remember being worried about her.

The service was about to begin. There was complete silence in the church. But then, suddenly, I heard someone running up the aisle. I turned around and saw it was the girl, running to her empty chair with her veil all crooked. I wondered why. Then I noticed that her mam wasn't there. The next thing was, this man walked up to the priest and whispered to him. The priest put a hand on his shoulder. The two men looked sad. Then the man walked back down the church, and the service began.

When the communion was over and we were all outside, the adults were chatting. I heard them say that the little girl's mam had died. She'd had a brain haemorrhage. I didn't know what that was, but it stuck in my mind. I never forgot it. But I had no sense of her spirit. Not then.

I carried on with my day. Mam and Dad brought me

visiting to all the relations. Then, later on, Dad brought me to the pub. I remember getting lots of money, but I don't remember any cards.

There was a spirit man in Foley Street. Nobody else was aware of him, though they must have sensed the air of gloom in that flat. I hadn't seen him when I met the little drowned boy, but I noticed him soon afterwards. He wasn't calm and still like the boy had been. This spirit was always grumpy. He was noisy, and I didn't like him one bit. He frightened me.

You would hear this constant crying. This moaning. I'd hear him all the time, but nobody else could hear him. I saw him too, many times. I got the feeling that nobody had ever liked him. He always seemed to be giving out. At least, he always gave out to me.

The whole flat was freezing. It was on ground level, and what I remember most is the damp and the cold. But the toilet was the worst. It was outside, beyond the tiny little kitchen. It was solid concrete with no plaster on the walls, let alone paint. There was no toilet paper either. We used newspapers that had been cut up.

I hated going out there. I'd try not to. I'd try with all my might, and by the time I gave in I'd be bursting. I'd run in then, as quickly as I could. And it wasn't just to avoid the cold. The spirit man would be there, waiting for me. I'd do anything to avoid him. He was horrible!

He'd shake his fist at me and shout, 'Go away, little girl. You're not allowed in here.'

I found him so scary. I don't know why the spirit man was like that. Maybe he didn't like anyone living in that flat. I think he felt it belonged to him.

Mam thought the flat was spooky. The whole family did,

but nobody except me had seen or heard the spirit man. But one night, all that changed.

My cousin Sean was staying in the flat – well, actually he was my uncle, but I never called him that. He was just five years older than me, and he often came so that his parents could go out for the night. I was sleeping on the sofa in the little sitting room, and Sean was on the floor beside me on a roll-up mattress. The spirit man started moaning. I remember hearing him, and Sean sat up.

'What was that?' He was terrified.

'Oh God.' I raised my eyes. 'It's the ghost.'

'The ghost? What ghost?' Sean lay back and pulled the grey blanket over his head. 'I'm not listening,' he said.

I could see the old man. His hair looked wild, and he was scowling even more than usual. I could see he was not happy with Sean. Not one little bit. He got hold of the blanket and pulled it, slowly, off Sean. Sean sat up again.

'Patricia! Stop it!' he said. Then he saw me sitting up on the sofa with my hands up over my eyes. He started to scream, and Mam came running. Sean looked so funny. He got such a fright, his hair was standing up. Mam had to take him into the big bedroom with her and Dad. And after that, he refused to sleep in our house. He never did, ever again. He was so, so scared.

Mam said the spirit man wasn't real. She said she thought I'd made him up and frightened Sean. But she did call out the priest. She got the flat blessed. And for a while the spirit man was quiet. But some time later, he was there and all angry again.

Life was always tough for our family. Always. Dad was almost impossible to live with. He was abusive, and there was always tension around him. He hadn't been able to cope with army discipline, yet in some ways the discipline of being in the military had rubbed off on him. It had made him really particular. Everything had to be in its place. He wanted perfection, and that's not easy when there are three young children around.

Another thing, he got up every morning at 5.30 and he made us all get up at that time too. That never changed with him.

And then, of course, he drank. Alcohol was always a problem with him. He'd come back from the pub, at eleven, or twelve, or whenever the pubs closed. And he expected his dinner to be on the table. This wasn't easy. There was, of course, no microwave. And worse, often there was no electricity either. Mam would have a pot of water, heated from the fire, and keep his dinner on a plate over the pot, with another plate on top of that. She did her best, but if the dinner was cold, Dad would always complain.

Sometimes, he would bring friends home – just anyone who had been in the bar. He'd want Mam to feed them too. He would make out to them that we had the food to spare, but we never did. Never ever. Mam would run round the kitchen looking for something. And she'd be so tired. Sometimes, Dad and his friends would play cards for the rest of the night.

It never seemed right to me that we had such a difficult life. We had lots of cousins. We'd see them often, and life was much better for them. I'd see them living well and having nice things. And we never did. We never ever had new clothes – everything we owned came in bags from St Vincent de Paul. I knew something wasn't right about our life, but I suppose I accepted it. That was just the way things were.

I always wanted my dad's love. I always wanted him to

feel proud of me. I always just wanted him to say, 'Well done.' But he didn't. It didn't matter what I did, he was never proud. He was always slapping me – well, he slapped all of us. I was scared of him. I was terrified of him, but I never hated him.

You never knew where you were with my dad. He'd be grand one minute, then all of a sudden he'd just explode into a rage. He was always bad when he was drunk. We learned to keep out of his way, but sometimes he'd wake up in a mood. You'd be asleep, and the first thing you'd know was your head hitting the floor. He'd get you by the ankle. You'd never know what would set him off. It could be the tiniest thing, like something out of place. If there was an unwashed cup lying around, even that would make him mad. He wanted everything to be perfect, and it was up to us to make sure that it was. That was the least he expected.

I didn't get a lot of love at home, but I got loads from my nan – my Nanny Bridget, my dad's mam. When I was little she would take me to her house in Ballyfermot. She'd take me as much as she could. I was blissfully happy there, but Dad didn't like me to visit. When he heard I was there, I was brought straight back.

Nan loved all of us, I know she did, but she and I had a special bond. That's because Nan understood about the angels. She was the same as me. She could see them too. Nan knew things. People would go to her house and sit at her kitchen table. She was very gentle. She didn't call herself a psychic or an angel woman, but she had, sometimes, given messages to people. She just never broadcast it.

I loved sitting on Nan's knee for a hug. She was nice and plump. She was tall too. Much taller than me, and she had silver hair. She came from Donegal. I loved her accent. I could listen to her all day. She never shouted. I loved that.

Everyone shouted at home, but Nan never raised her voice. She never said a bad word about anything. Her motto was: If you can't say something good, don't say anything at all.

And Nan loved looking after people. She had a potion for everything. She'd been a nurse before she got married, and she was a midwife too. So when there were babies being born, Nan was always sent for.

Nan and Granddad had a mixed marriage. Granddad was a devout Catholic, but Nan was a Protestant. It wasn't an issue with them. When they got married, Nan had to agree that she'd bring up their children as Catholics. She was happy to do that.

When I was there, I'd be going to Mass with Granddad every morning. Nan thought that was a bit much. She was always asking him why he'd bring me, when I was so little. But I liked it. I liked going with him. He was lovely to me always. He was like a gentle giant.

I loved my other grandparents too; my mam's parents. But they were very, very different. Mam's mam, Nanny Chris, was modern. She didn't seem old. She was funny. She dressed smartly. I remember her wearing tight-fitting skirts and a trench coat. She'd pull the belt of the trench coat in really tight, to show off her tiny waist.

Nanny Chris didn't walk like other people. She'd kind of sway down the street like a model. If we ran after her and shouted, 'Nanny Chris!' she'd shush us.

'Don't call me Nanny Chris,' she'd say. 'I'm too young to be a nanny! Just call me Chrissie.' And she *did* look young for her age. She was hilarious. She was very into beauty. Perhaps that was because she was half Italian. I remember her showing me how to push my cuticles back so that my nails would look good. She was always going on about the importance of moisturizer too. And she was always fun. When she wanted to show us she cared for us, she'd give us money. That was her way. With Nan it was a hug. They were two very different characters, but one thing was for sure. They both loved us very much.

Just after I made my first holy communion I had my seventh birthday. I don't really remember it. I would love to remember. I don't think I had a cake. That might have been because Mam's fourth baby was due in a month or so. Maybe she was just too tired.

By the time I was seven, I was becoming more aware of the angels around me. They'd started to speak to me, and they always protected me. I had this feeling of really great love from them. But I never told Mam about any of this. I couldn't. Not after the way she had reacted about the little boy. That bothered me, because the angels were my friends.

It was really difficult. We'd get back from school, and she'd ask me what I'd done all day. My main news, always, was playing with the angels. So not sharing it was hard.

One day, Mam was in the bedroom and the angels said to me, 'Call your mam from the bedroom.'

I didn't ask them why they wanted me to do that. I knew they liked to protect me, so I just did as they asked.

'Mam!' I shouted. 'Mam, can you come here please?'

'Not now, Patricia. I can't. I'm busy.'

'Please, Mam.' I was desperate. I knew, somehow, that it was important that she came.

'It'll have to wait, whatever it is. I'm busy here. I'm clearing this room for the new baby.'

At that moment I heard this terrible crash. Mam screamed. I ran into the room and saw that the bed had fallen on top of Mam. She was crying out. I was terrified. I ran next door, and the lady and her husband came round and managed to get Mam out. She looked really pale and she was shaken. Someone called an ambulance, and she was taken off to hospital. I was very upset. Especially as the angels had seen what would happen. I felt bad that I'd been warned, but had not been able to stop the accident. The angels could see I was upset. They opened their wings and wrapped them around me.

'Your mam will be OK,' they said. 'Don't worry about her. She'll be home with you soon.'

They were right. Mam did come home. But the baby she was expecting didn't. He never lived. He went home to the angels.

Mam was so sad. She was heartbroken. She started going in on herself. I think the grief must have given her depression. Maybe she was always depressed. That made it difficult for her to express love for her children. I always wished that she could, but she never seemed able to cope. I suppose being married to Dad was enough to wear her down even before the baby died.

2 Manchester

The angels can't stop bad things happening. But they
can stop you from feeling the pain.

Before my ninth birthday, we moved to England yet again.
This time we lived in Manchester. We had the top flat in a
big, old-fashioned house. The house had a huge long hallway, and upstairs, on the fourth landing, was a kitchen which
all the flats shared. The door to our flat was beside this. We
lived in this huge room. There was a TV in there, and the
table we ate at, but also Mam and Dad's big double bed. It
swamped the room. As for myself, Liz and John – we slept
up in the attic.

I remember that time. I remember the Manchester streets.
They were cobbled and narrow – just like you see on *Coron-
ation Street*. And there's one day I will never ever forget, not as
long as I live. I was sent on an errand to the shop at the end
of my road. I had to go and buy bread and milk for Dad's tea
and I had to get back before he arrived home from work. If
I was late there would be hell to pay. But Mam had only sent
me at the last minute. I knew I might be late, so I was in a
terrible hurry.

I was going as fast as I could but I was wearing Mam's
shoes. I'd been trying them on, when she shouted at me to
go to the shop. I'd taken them without asking, and I ran out
of the house before she could see I was wearing them. I kept

slipping in them because, of course, they were much too big for my little feet.

The shoes were bright and shiny and brand new. I loved them the second I saw my mam with them. I felt all grown up as I clattered down the street. It was hard to keep them on, though. It took a lot of concentration. And when I stepped out between two parked cars, my head was down, looking at the shoes, and I didn't see the car coming.

I don't remember being hit. But I do remember being gently lifted in many arms. To this day I can feel the warm embrace as I was carried carefully across the street and laid on the footpath. I was lifted by neighbours, but there were angels there too. They put their wings around me. I remember the softness and security. I was quiet and still. Nothing moved. Then there were people around me looking down. I could see their lips moving but I couldn't hear what they were saying.

All that was worrying me was that the money had gone. I'd had coins in my hand, and now I hadn't. I was worried about the shoes too. Where had they gone? As I was being picked up and put into a neighbour's car, I spotted one lying further along the path. I could also see the other one out on the road in front of the car. Seeing them lying there and knowing I had lost the money frightened me more than anything else.

At the hospital I was examined and released after an hour. The doctors were baffled. They told my parents they could find no sign of an injury. I had been struck by the car, of that there was no doubt. The driver was distraught. He was in shock when he spoke to my parents. He said he'd had no chance to avoid me – I'd stepped out right in front of him. So why was I completely unhurt? There were no broken bones. No pain. I didn't even have a cut or a bruise. There wasn't a mark on me.

I knew that it was the angels who had saved me. They were already as real to me and as much a part of my life as my parents and my brother and sister. But that was the moment when I realized just how important they were to me. They had now become a powerful source in my life.

I first met Archangel Michael when I was nine, and from that first day I began to have a very strong bond with him. When he came there was this bright light – it was so pure that it would take my breath away.

I remember, shortly after I'd first seen the Archangel Michael, I was on my way back from the shops, when I saw a black comb on the ground. I was terrified. I'd heard that a comb was a sign of the banshee. I stopped dead and jumped away from it – I think I expected it to jump up and follow me. I wasn't looking where I was going, and was about to run off the pavement. But suddenly Archangel Michael was there. He stood in front of me, so I had to stop.

He said, 'There's no such thing as a banshee. There is evil, but there's not a banshee. And anyway, Patricia, I will always protect you.'

When I was a child, I liked to comfort people and to help them. My mother called me the 'there there' child. That's because if someone was hurting, I would go up to them and say, 'There there.' I just felt it was the right thing to do. I later learned from the angels that I had unconditional love inside me. That's why I couldn't bear to see other people's pain. I would feel their pain. Literally. It would hurt.

Dad was a very strict man. We were terrified of him and always did what we were told. It was very hard confined with him in that flat. He got a job, but he would go to the pub every night. When he was drunk he could be very violent. And he didn't like it if my brother, my sister and myself made any noise.

A couple with two children lived next door. They were friendly. I will call them the Jacksons, but that's not their real name. Mr Jackson played with us a lot, but there was always something funny about his play. He'd sit me on his knee, and he'd bounce me up and down. He'd tickle me, and sometimes it didn't feel good. It made me feel uncomfortable, though I didn't know why.

Anyway, they got on really well with Mam and Dad, and the four of them would go out together – just to the pub across the road. The Jacksons' children were small then. One was a toddler, and the other was just a few weeks old. So when they went out, the two babies would sleep in the big room with me, and the grown-ups would take it in turns to come across the road to check that they were OK.

One night I was watching TV in my mam's bed when the door opened and Mr Jackson walked in. It was his turn to check on the babies. I remember him coming into the room, looking at me strangely. And I remember that the angels had gathered. I could see them behind him. I remember finding that odd.

'Everything's fine,' I said. 'The babies have been really good.'

'I can see that,' he said. 'But now I've got to check on you.'

'No, you don't!' I laughed. 'I'm not a baby. I'm nine. And I'm OK. I'm fine.'

He pulled back the covers of the bed, and climbed in beside me. I couldn't think what he was doing that for. As I looked at him, behind him I could see my angels looking sad.

I was looking at them and they were crying. He started to touch me then, and it didn't feel right. I didn't like it.

'You've got to be a good girl,' he said, and his hands were moving all over me. I told him to stop. But he went on, and told me I had to be good or my dad would be upset. I was quiet then, because we always had to be careful not to upset my dad.

I didn't understand what was happening. I just knew that I didn't like the things he was doing to me. Eventually he stopped. He got up, checked his appearance in the mirror, then he just went off and told me I wasn't to tell anybody.

'If you tell anyone, you'll get into big trouble.' He held my elbow and called me a bold child. 'I mean it. You know what your dad is like.' We were terrified of Dad. When he'd gone I was still crying. I found I couldn't stop.

The angels said, 'We can't protect you from what he is doing. But we can stop you feeling the pain.' And they did. I felt safe. I was in a bubble, and from there, I couldn't feel or hear what was going on.

After that I'd dread those nights when they'd all go out because every time Mr Jackson was the one coming back and checking. Every time. He offered and the others were happy to let him. And each time he would touch me more, and it felt so wrong.

Then Dad had to go off somewhere, and Mam decided she wanted to go out. Mam was often going out in England. Two of her sisters lived there, and she was happy. She saw them a lot – she'd even get her hair done.

That time she wanted to stay out for a good long while, so Mr Jackson said, 'Sure, I'll look after the kids.'

That gave him more time with me. By now he was making me touch him too. He made me do things to him. And I didn't dare say no. The abuse went on and on. And then one day, about a year and a half later, Mam got a house off the council.

It was a beautiful house, and I was so happy. And not just because it was a house and not just a room. It felt like it was miles away – away from the flat and from the Jacksons. I felt so safe there. I made friends and went to school. For a year, everything was wonderful. Then, guess what? They got a house too. I'll never forget that day when Mam told me.

'Isn't it great?' she said. 'It will be so good having them near again.' And they were near. If you looked out of our kitchen window you could see their house, right there. Mr Jackson still came over to babysit, but, worse, I had to go to his house too. I'd go there to babysit his children. And that's when the abuse got really, really bad. He was forcing himself on me. I was just ten years old. I don't remember the pain. Not now. I blocked it out, and the angels were there to make it better. But I do remember one time when he made me bleed. I was really sore. I cried, and didn't know what to do.

'Don't tell your mam,' he said.

'I have to. It hurts!'

'Then tell her you fell off your bike.'

I did, but Dad didn't understand that. 'How could that make her bleed between her legs?' he asked. I didn't know what to say. I just went red. But Mr Jackson was there with me, as cool as you like.

'Oh, she got caught on the handlebars,' he said. And Dad accepted that. He took me to the hospital. He was really worried about me.

I remember this nurse in the hospital. She said, 'How did you fall off your bike?' She was asking me all sorts. I was terrified. Terrified she'd learn the truth.

The angels were saying, 'Tell her. Tell her.'

But in my head I was hearing Mr Jackson saying, 'Your dad will kill yer. Your dad will kill yer.' And I couldn't. The angels wrapped themselves around me. My angels were the thing that kept me going. It is so hard to describe the comfort and the love that they gave me. Hard to describe it to anyone who doesn't see angels themselves. They helped me to be a strong person. They literally rocked me. And they *did* comfort me. When I cried my angels cried. It made me sad to see them cry but they did. Because they couldn't take away my pain.

What they said to me was, 'You are going to have a hard life.' I knew I was going to have a hard life but they told me I'd get through it. They told me that one day I would realize why. It was many years later when I did realize why. I can actually help someone who has been through sexual abuse. I do believe that. I can really understand. When somebody mentions that they have been abused as a child, I can understand because I know what it feels like. Because it happened to me.

The abuse went on. And one day, when I was eleven, just before we moved back to Ireland, I told Mam. I remember that day so well. Dad had got me these red clogs from Holland. I loved those clogs. We weren't allowed to wear them to school, but I actually wore them that day. All you could hear was this clip clop, clip clop. I got into trouble with the nuns. I was hauled up in front of the whole school, because the clogs weren't part of the uniform. I didn't care. I just wanted people to see I'd got red clogs from a different country. It made me feel special, and that was a feeling I didn't often have.

Later, at home, I still had those clogs on. And I had on a

red top to match. I was standing on the stairs looking down at Mam, who was in the hall. It was one of the times I felt really sore because of the abuse. I was hurting and I was crying. Mam asked me what was wrong and I thought, *This is my chance to tell her.* So I told her about Mr Jackson. I told her that I didn't like what he was doing to me. I said that he was hurting me.

'What do you mean?'

I cried even harder. 'I'm very sorry, Mam. I was bold, but I do not like Mr Jackson.'

I don't know why I said that I was bold. Perhaps because the Jacksons were Mam and Dad's closest friends, and so she'd be upset. Or maybe because part of me believed Mr Jackson when he said it was all my fault; that I *was* a bold girl. I don't know what I expected her to do, but I was sure she wouldn't want me hurting. I will never forget it. That split second she slapped me. It was such a shock.

She said, 'Don't you ever say anything like that about him, because he's a very nice man and he would never hurt you.'

I was in shock. I realized she didn't believe me. She thought I was making it up, just as she thought I made it up when I told her I was seeing the angels.

Then I began to think that maybe Mr Jackson was right. And maybe it was me that made him do what he did, because that's what he said to me. He'd say, 'It's because of you I do this. You know that.'

So when Mam slapped me that day, I believed that. I thought, *He is right, it is because of me. Because of me I have upset Mam.* I'd never been able to really talk to Mam. Not really talk. It was always, 'Patricia, you're the big girl. I need you to help me clean up.'

I always felt that I was a cause for Mam's unhappiness.

Mam and Dad would argue and I'd always hear the same from Dad. 'If you hadn't got pregnant I wouldn't have married you.'

So that made me feel bad. I figured I'd made my Mam's life miserable. Because of me she'd had beatings to put up with. That went through my mind a lot.

I never really forgot that slap. I always felt Mam could have done something about the abuse. I do believe that had she told Dad that day, Mr Jackson would have gone to prison. But she didn't mention it to anyone.

Dad would have done something. I know in my heart he would have. He might have been physically abusive, but there was one thing he was always finicky about – anything to do with the sexual abuse of children. He'd kill anyone if he thought they were going to touch a child.

I didn't know it then, but soon the abuse would stop anyway. It went on for a bit, but soon after that we moved back to Ireland. In some ways that was such a relief. In other ways, though, that was sad.

There were happy times in Manchester too. Wonderful times. I loved school – I passed all my exams. I loved learning because I liked to know things. I had one friend, Marian, in England. She was the first friend I made when we moved to the new house. She lived round the corner and she had two little brothers. I remember they all watched our furniture going in. She asked me my name and asked me if I was going to the same school as her. I said I didn't know, because I didn't know what school I was going to.

I ended up at her school, St Patrick's School in Manchester. I was in the same class as her, and we stuck together like superglue. We had that connection, a really, really strong connection. We made our confirmation together – it's really weird: in England when you made your confirmation you wore a white dress and veil. It felt like I was making my communion all over again. On our confirmation day they asked Marian and me to walk up the church aisle together.

We were in every class together. I loved all the classes, especially English and art. I loved essays and everything about writing, and I loved the art classes. I loved colour, and making things, and creating my own designs. I still do it today; I'm not especially good at it, but it relaxes me.

Marian knew about the angels. She'd ask me about them, especially when we were in class and doing religion. We got separated a few times in class, because of talking. She'd whisper, 'Can you see the angels now?'

I'd see them in the corner of the classroom. They'd be round the children. Like a shimmering light, but I could see the shapes. These days I can see all the different angels, but as a child I couldn't tell them apart. I could just see angels. Marian loved to hear about angels. I do believe maybe Marian herself might have had that connection.

It was a short-lived friendship, but Marian and I were so close. There were lots of children on the estate but she was the one I played with. I often think about Marian. When I was with her I didn't think about the abuse. I never thought about anything, only playing. We had our games, we'd giggle together. We laughed and giggled so much. We were very happy the way children should be. That was two years of intense childhood.

3 Growing Up

Our Lady has a light that shines, and makes you feel
all warm inside.

We arrived back from England in the summer when I was eleven. It was good, in ways, to be back. It was nice to be near all my grandparents again. We had a house now. A house with a garden, and it was in a nice street too. That was an improvement on before. It was a corporation house in Edenmore on the Northside of Dublin. For all that, coming back to Ireland was heartbreaking in a way. My childhood was gone. The abuse had stopped, but life wasn't perfect.

For one thing, money was always short. When Dad had a bit of work, which he often did, the money went on drink. Or maybe on the horses – he liked a bet. It was always the same. Sometimes we had to beg for food. We'd walk all the way from Edenmore, maybe as far as Crumlin on the Southside, which was a distance of about eight miles. We'd stop at any convent that was on the way, where we'd go in to get a bit of food. This would be me and John, Mam, and sometimes the latest baby, Mark, as well. He was still small, so he'd come in his pushchair. Sometimes he stayed behind with Liz. She didn't like coming with us.

On the way back, if it wasn't raining, Mam would say, 'Can youse look for cigarette butts?' They weren't for her. Mam never smoked or drank. They were for Dad. We would bring a plastic bag with us. We'd make it into a game, and would see who could find the biggest cigarette butt. We'd usually manage to fill the plastic bag, and when we got home my mam would take all the tobacco out of the butts and put it in a tin. My dad would use it for rolled cigarettes.

I remember one day that summer, Dad sent myself, Liz and John out into the back garden. It was like a jungle out there, with all the thick grass and the weeds.

He gave us each a pair of blunt scissors, and said, 'Get out there and cut the grass. And don't think of coming back inside again until it's all done.'

I remember it was damp out there. And it was hard, hard work. After a while my hand went into a cramp. I went on, cutting and cutting, but my sister and John started messing. And that's when the man next door, Mr Duff, noticed us.

'What are you doing out there?' he asked.

'Cutting the grass,' I said. I wondered why he'd asked, since it must've been obvious. He was really nice.

'That must be hard work,' he said, and I agreed it was. I said that we were doing it for our dad.

He went inside then, and he told Dad it was a disgrace that he made us do that. We could hear him shouting. And Dad made some excuse. He called us in then, and spoke to us really nicely in front of Mr Duff. I was so pleased. He seemed so grateful for the work we'd done. But as soon as Mr Duff had gone, every one of us got a hiding. He didn't care. All he cared about was that we'd allowed Mr Duff to see us.

'You fucking showed me up,' he said, as he gave us a clatter.

Mam loved Dad. And when he wasn't drunk, he could be a real charmer. He always looked good too, and he could be funny. He could be a wonderful man. For everything he did to me, I never hated him. I never ever said, 'I hate you.'

There were happy times in my childhood. That was if Dad was in good form; if he came home from the pub and the fire was blazing because we had coal. Sometimes he got into militarized mode. That was funny. He'd get out the sweeping brush and teach us how to stand to attention. He'd pretend the brush was a gun. You had to make the brush tap the floor with your left hand; then you'd bring it up straight, pass it to your right hand, and place it on your left shoulder. And that was it. That was your attention done. He loved making us do that. But we had to do it right – if we didn't, we could get a right old clatter. I think he missed the army.

Sometimes Dad would take us into town. If he did, he always brought us into the pub. He'd buy us a big glass bottle of red lemonade to share. He'd get us some glasses and that would last us. I remember I loved the ice going in. I loved the way it made the lemonade fizz. I remember my stomach would feel full afterwards from all the gas. John would burp, and we'd all fall about laughing.

I was looking forward to going back to school after the summer. I should have been starting in secondary school, but Mam never enrolled me. I didn't attend school at all after the age of twelve. I never understood why. The authorities never came to find out why I wasn't at school. When I was older I thought about that, and I found it strange.

My brothers and sisters all went to secondary school. Sometimes I felt jealous of them; especially of my sister, Liz. She stayed at school until she was sixteen, and I felt I should have been there too. But I didn't say it to Mam. I accepted it. I knew that Mam relied on me to help with the younger children as they came along. It was just the way it was.

My dad didn't even know at first. He thought I was in school. He wanted me there. He always believed that education was important, and he was fussy about it. I think, now, that's because he was always mitching school. Mam made me pretend that I was in school. I'd even put on a uniform when Dad was there, and I'd change in the coal room before I left for work.

My first job, when I was twelve, was down Kilbarrack in the supermarket. The job was stacking shelves. Back then, you had to be fifteen before you were allowed to work, so I had to try and make myself look older. I got the biggest pair of platform shoes I could to give me height. I'm not into make-up. I'm not now and I wasn't back then, but I'd put it on anyway. I'd do anything that would make me look older.

I had been working in the supermarket for several months and I remember one day I was up on a step, stacking shelves, and the angels came to me and said, 'You're going to be in big trouble later on today.'

I looked at them strangely. 'Why?' I said. 'Why would I be in trouble? I'm working hard here. I'm not doing anything wrong.'

'Your dad is going to be coming through the shopping centre.'

That didn't make any sense to me. Why would he do that? But it turned out they were right. He'd been looking for work, and he'd got himself a job as a security man in the same shopping centre. I couldn't believe it when I saw him coming in. I tried to hide, but I found I couldn't move. I froze.

Dad was in uniform. My boss was bringing him round, showing him the ropes. As they were walking through the supermarket, I could hear Dad's voice boom out. I remember thinking, *Oh God, I'm in trouble now. What will I do?* I thought if I just stayed where I was, maybe he wouldn't recognize me. But just at that precise moment, the manager called me.

'Hey you!' He often couldn't remember my name. 'Could you stop stacking that shelf and get yourself down to the fruit and veg?'

I didn't move.

'Move it!' He was shouting now. 'We haven't got all day. We've had a delivery there, and there're a load of boxes to sort out.'

I didn't answer him. I didn't dare. I stayed where I was and kept my face hidden from him. I just would not turn round.

And my dad said, 'I wouldn't have staff like that working for me.'

My heart just sank. I remember thinking it was either turn round and face the consequences from Dad, or lose the job. So I got off the step and tried to slide past. But I heard Dad gasp, and when I glanced up, I saw his mouth hanging open. I've never seen him so shocked. The rest of the afternoon passed in a blur. When it was clocking-off time Dad was still there.

He said to me, 'I'll deal with you when I get home.'

'Dad, please don't be angry at me.'

'Your mother was supposed to bring you to school. Why are you not at school, why are you here?'

And I told a lie again. I said, 'Mam doesn't know. She thinks I'm in school,' but Mam knew. Of course she did. I gave her my money every week.

Dad nodded his head sadly, and said, 'Well, you've gone and done it now.'

I left the supermarket before a year was up. I had to, because after a year they'd be looking for forms and checking my age.

After that, I worked in a stationery and toy shop next door. I liked it there, too. By now, my dad kind of accepted that I worked. I suppose he thought, *Well, she's bringing in money anyway*.

Life was really tough when I was in my teens. Every day it was home from work to help Mam with the kids. Around that time Mam seemed to be always pregnant or not well. After my brother died, she didn't have any children for a while. There are seven years between John and my next brother down, Mark. He was born in England. She was managing, just, but the house was always a mess. Mam would sit in a chair. And she was always crying. She must have been a young woman still, but she looked old. And she never bothered about the way she looked.

In England, her sister Ursula was always taking her off to get her hair done. She never bothered with that when she came home. She didn't bother with make-up either. She'd never worn much, now she didn't even cleanse her face. I suppose she didn't have the money. Her mam, Nanny Chris, used to despair of her. She was always giving out to Mam. She'd say, 'Nancy, what are you doing? Why are you letting yourself go like that? For God's sake, I've got clothes in the wardrobe that are more modern than what you've got on now.'

Nanny Chris was right. Mam dressed as a woman much older than she was. One thing, she always wore bright colours; never black. But she didn't coordinate her clothes. She might wear a bright blue skirt and a yellow cardigan. She'd wear a skirt, a blouse and a cardigan buttoned up to her neck.

Mam never went out. She never went to bingo, the way all the neighbours did. She used to say that she wasn't allowed to go, but I never heard Dad tell her she couldn't. I don't really understand what it was with her. It was strange. Maybe Dad was very jealous. Perhaps he really couldn't bear to see Mam going out. That's the only conclusion I can come to, and because of that she retreated.

I think, now, that she must have been deeply depressed. After all, she had a lot of children. And an alcoholic husband, who was not always working. She had a really hard time. He could be abusive and controlling too. We all saw it. He'd go from work, if he had any, straight to the pub. But she wasn't allowed to go to bed until he came in. And then, more often than not, he'd be abusive. He's start at her again.

Edenmore was a corporation area, but there were privately owned houses there too, and most people on the road weren't as badly off as we were. In most households, the father worked and brought the money home to the wife and children. Dad worked, on and off, but he took the money to the pub or the bookies. A bit would come home, but not an awful lot. Two days out of the week, we would probably have a decent dinner. For the rest of it, then, you might have to live on porridge. And as the week went on, the porridge got weaker and weaker, because there wasn't enough, so you just added water. That's just the way it was.

The women on the road wanted to get to know Mam. They were lovely women. People can be very good. They'd pop in and see Mam, and if the electric hadn't been paid and everything was a mess, they didn't bat an eye to it. They'd say, 'Send me up a wash and I'll do it in my house.' It was never a thing of shame. They accepted her and her situation for what it was. They handled money better, that was all. They might borrow a fiver until pay day, then they paid it back. Just their houses were always somehow better than ours. Ours seemed to be a strange house.

I often wonder, looking back, why Mam put up with Dad. I wondered why she didn't just leave him.

I've asked her and she'd say, 'Oh, I put up with him, because of youse.' It was always 'youse', not 'my children'.

Mind you, there were times during our childhood when Mam had had enough. She'd leave Dad, and take us all with her. We'd be away a week or two, living in a refuge. We would be fine there and happy. Then Dad would come, and Mam would take us home.

I love Mam, and I always did love her, but I wished, back then, that she could have shown me more love. You basically had to fend for yourself, and that was it. I think she would have done anything for the sake of peace. Once Dad wasn't around, it was better. She was quite happy.

Mam expected us to do lots of work; and especially me. When the electricity was turned off, as it often was, we cooked on an open fire with a grate that you put a pot on. You'd push that pot into the fire. And we had a big kettle thing. I'd fill that and push it into the fire for hot water. When the bill was paid, the electricity would be on. When it wasn't, we relied on that fire for everything.

We were all supposed to help, and there were always arguments over who was going to do what. My sister's job was supposed to be the kitchen, but by the time she got round to that, I'd have the kitchen cleaned anyway. I did more than all my sisters and brothers. I'm like that, and I'm still like that to this day. I'm very much a get-up-and-go person. Nothing keeps me down.

It was a happy house sometimes, like the times when Dad was out and all the kids played. I remember sometimes we made a stage. I enjoyed that, because I was using my creative side. I would do a puppet show; I'd stitch buttons onto socks. I always loved making people happy.

Sometimes Dad would come home and see what I was doing. Sometimes it would make him laugh. He'd be happy. There were times, even, when I thought that, just for a minute, he was proud of me. That made me so happy. I wished it could always be like that.

I loved music, especially rock and roll. I still do. I loved Elvis Presley, the Beatles and the Everly Brothers. Music changes me completely. It makes me feel alive.

The angels were always around for me. I heard them around the children, when things were happy. They'd be clapping. I tried to protect the younger ones as much as I could. I didn't want them to suffer. After Mark, Margaret and Bridget, there was Debbie, then Lisa. I didn't want them to go through the hurt and hunger that I went through, and the younger three were more protected than the rest of us.

Dad didn't improve, but he didn't hit the younger ones. I didn't let him, so he hit the older ones instead. It was, 'I'll take it for you.' You get so used to clatters it goes over you. It was like a really hard slap. But the slap wasn't the worst of it. You'd come home sometimes and find him in a rage. He'd be off. There'd be no talking to him. He'd throw everything out of the window and we'd have to pick it up. And if it was broken it would be, 'Well, fix it then.' He didn't care. And we got used to it. That was the life.

It was hard, but I understand now that it wasn't his fault. It wasn't my mam's fault either. I do believe she was bright and bubbly when she met my dad. I really do believe that. But after having all those children it wore her down.

Life would have been harder for me were it not for the angels. They would help me so much. And they would tell me the things I needed to hear. They comforted me, always. It was strange for me when I realized not everyone could see them; not even the Archangel Michael. He was always there for me.

My brother Mark couldn't talk. He didn't make any sounds, even when he was a toddler. One day, a nun from the convent came to the house, and asked Mam would she like to take Mark to Lourdes. Mam shook her head.

'I haven't the money,' she said. 'It's just impossible.'

As I looked at her I could see two angels standing side by side. Their wings were wrapped round Mam, and I could see a beautiful pink light around her. But she was so sad. Mam was so sad. She was trapped in her own world. I know she wished she could do more for all her children.

'You should go, Mam,' I said.

'Oh yes, Patricia. And how am I to pay for it?'

'The money will come.'

Putting her hand on her hips, Mam gave me one of her looks. 'Right,' she said, with a sigh. And I knew what she was thinking. Here she was with an alcoholic husband, five children at that stage, no money and no food. I think she saw it as no life.

When I told Mam the money would come, the angels smiled at me and said, 'Don't worry, Patricia, everything will be OK.'

And it was. When the nun realized money was a problem, she told Mam that the church would pay the fare for her and Mark to go to Lourdes. I was jumping up and down with excitement when I heard. But Mam saw a problem.

'That's all very well,' Mam said. 'But how will we manage when we're there? We'll be there for five days. I need spending money too. And where do you suppose *that* is going to come from?'

I realized then that it was up to me. I had to get the money for Mam. I thought long and hard, and then I came up with an idea. I gave in my notice at work. That meant I got paid a back week – and I got extra money for holiday pay. It wasn't a lot. It was about seventeen pounds, but back then seventeen pounds was a lot of money. It made all the difference, and they were able to go.

I didn't tell my dad I'd handed in my notice. If I had he would have killed me. Even though he hadn't, at first, liked the idea of me working, by now he was used to the money coming in. So I told him I'd got the week off work to help look after the children. He was happy enough with that.

Mam and Mark went to Lourdes. I worried about them going, but the angels told me they would be OK. They said I mustn't worry.

'But what is it like at Lourdes?' I always had a very strong connection to Our Lady. I still do. I saw her then as a nice lady whose light would shine and make you feel all warm inside. I longed to be with Mam and my brother, but while they were away the angels and I had great conversations about heaven. They told me I was a very old soul and had been back to earth many times, and that this was my last time on earth.

'You will go through many hard times, but you will come through. And you're to remember that, whatever happens, the angels are always with you.' I didn't fully understand what they meant.

I couldn't wait for Mam and Mark to come home. When they did, I remember looking at Mark. Just looking at him. I was waiting for the words to come out of his mouth. Just anything. Any words. But he didn't speak. I was really disappointed.

I asked Mam, 'Can Mark talk now? Did Our Lady make him better?' I couldn't believe nothing had changed. I was full of questions. He didn't look any different to before.

The angels laughed at me then. They said I was too impatient.

'Healing takes time,' they said. 'Our Lady has given Mark his healing, and he will eventually speak. It's a gradual process.'

Mam looked different already though. It was like someone had switched a light on in the room. She looked radiant. She had a glow around her that I had never seen before. As I looked at her again the angels were all around her. I now believe Mam got healing at Lourdes. I believe that is why she was called to go. She badly needed healing and she got it.

Mam never talked to me about what happened to her in Lourdes. But she seemed happy when she came home. It was like she was no longer hurting inside. When she came home, and for a while afterwards, she became carefree. It didn't matter if Dad came home in a drunken mood, she still seemed happy. But after a while she got dragged down again.

She tried making a kind of altar. I was really happy about that. She brought home this special disc with a hole in it.

'What's this?' I asked.

'It's special. If you look through the hole for ten seconds, then look up at the ceiling, an image of Our Lady will appear.'

I thought that was great. I tried it and I saw the image. Then I started crying.

'Why are you crying?'

'Because Our Blessed Lady has entered the room.'

Mam's reaction surprised me. She said, 'Don't be so stupid. That's just an illusion.' But for me it meant so much.

I still can't explain why I had this fascination with Our Lady. It was never spoken about at home. Never. Ours wasn't a religious house. My Dad sent us to Mass, all right, but he never came with us. I think he sent us just for show.

I was always different from the others. John called me

Holy Mary! I'd look at the others, at how laid-back they were, and I'd think I'd been adopted.

I'd say to Mam, 'Are you sure I'm your daughter? Could I have been mixed with someone else?'

She'd say, 'You must be mine. You have to be, because you were born at home.'

I waited and waited for Mark to talk. I waited two years. Mark was three and a half. I was working all the time by then, and one day I brought home meat and vegetables from Moore Street Market. I was standing in the kitchen talking to Mam and showing her the meat.

'We can make a grand big pot of stew,' I said. John was there too, I remember. And Margaret and Bridget were on the floor playing with dolls. They were making an almighty racket, and the radio was blasting out as well. I loved the radio; I loved dancing to it, but often we had no batteries.

John offered to help with the stew.

'That would be grand,' I said, handing him the bag of spuds. 'Would you ever wash these?' He took the spuds and headed for the sink. John was always helpful. But then he knew I'd reward him. If I had money left, I'd always buy him sweets.

Just then Dad came home. He tripped over Margaret, and kicked her doll out of his way.

'What the fuck is that doing there?" Dad switched off the radio. 'Jaysus,' he said, and I knew he was in one of his moods. He was drunk again. We all sensed it. Margaret was screaming, but Bridget just froze. She didn't want Dad to notice her.

John and I began to cut up the vegetables. I was silently asking the angels to please make this a happy day. They came into the room and I smiled at them. I felt safe when they were around. The room just lit up.

Dad started giving out to Mam. He was going on about the time, years ago in England, when Mam hadn't posted the pools coupon. We did it every week, but she thought it was a waste of money. That week Dad's numbers came up. He came running in shouting that we were rich! He picked Mam up and swung her round, and he went around telling everyone about his big win. After a day or two she had to tell him. He'd never forgiven her. And every time he was on the drink he would bring it up.

Just then I noticed Mark sitting under the table. He grabbed me by the leg, and as I bent down to him, I noticed two angels under the table with him.

'I forgot all about you!'

He smiled, and then he spoke. He said, 'Ya Ya.' It wasn't much. I didn't know what he meant, but it was the first time, ever, we'd heard him speak. It had been a long wait. The angels appeared then. They were smiling.

'See, Patricia?' they said. 'We told you Mark would talk. Are you happy now?' Was I! I picked Mark up then, and he said it again.

'Ya Ya.' This time he had a big smile on his face.

I said, 'You're great, Mark. You're so clever to talk!'

Dad had stopped shouting. He and Mam had been struck dumb. They heard him too, and the row was forgotten. Drunk as Dad was, there were tears in his eyes. I'll never forget that day.

After that I'd teach Mark new words every day. And from then on a lot of the time I was called Yaya. I still am.

4 Early Teenage Years

Every day I pray for peace; and for people to turn
away from evil.

When Mam and Mark first came back from Lourdes, I stayed
hanging around the house, helping Mam with the children,
and hoping Mark might speak. But Mam and Mark had barely
been home a day when Dad went on at me, asking why I was
still at home. I couldn't go back to the stationery and toy
shop, because I'd given in my notice. So I got myself ready,
and off I went out to see if I could find another job. I spent
the whole day in town looking for work, but I couldn't find
anything. On my way back on the bus I was very upset,
wondering what would happen to us all.

A girl got on at the next stop. She sat beside me and we
got chatting. It turned out she didn't live far from me. She
had also been looking for work. I told her that I'd been in
town all day, and that I'd found nothing.

'How old are you?' she asked. I almost said twelve, nearly
thirteen, which was my real age, but I decided to lie.

'I'm fifteen.'

'Oh, right. So am I,' she said. 'Well, there is work in
Donabate. It's not ideal. It's strawberry picking, and it does
your back in. And that's not the worst of it. To get there you
have to get the train at six every morning.'

I asked her all about it and she said I could just turn up.

I thought I might as well give it a try. I got up the next morning at five, just to be sure I would make it to the train. I remember walking up the road in the deathly quiet. There wasn't a soul around. I thought of everyone still tucked up in their beds. I liked the quiet. I could hear birds just starting to sing. It was all so peaceful. As I walked along, the angels were right there beside me. I loved the angels more than anything in the world. I was chatting away to them, asking them what my day would be like.

'It will be hard,' they said. 'You'll find the work tough, but it will also be fulfilling.' When I got to the station, the platform for the Donabate train was crowded with people. That's because this was an ideal summer job. And the great thing was, it didn't matter that I was still young. Nobody would ever check. As long as we could pick strawberries and get them into a punnet – that was all that mattered.

We got off the train and onto a bus. I always managed to get a seat, so I always got work. They gave us these big white containers to put the strawberries in. You'd fill one, then fill another and stack them on top of each other. Then we had to bring them all the way back down the field to a shed. The strawberries were weighed there, and we got paid depending on the weight. It wasn't a lot of money, but the good thing was, you got paid there and then. You didn't have to wait for the weekend.

It was really tough work. All the bending made my back terribly sore. But for all that, I loved it. The sun was shining. We were outdoors. The happiness that was around those fields was just brilliant. Everyone got on with everyone else, and we helped each other out. If someone had finished before you, they'd come and help you.

When we stopped for lunch, everybody shared. We were

all there for one reason. Just to earn a few bob. I would go back again today if I could. I loved being in the open air.

It was absolutely great. We had a lot of fun. We spent a lot of time messing and throwing strawberries at each other, then we'd realize if we did that, we wouldn't get paid as much. So we'd concentrate on picking the strawberries again. Whatever else, I was really proud of myself for getting out there and finding work. It gave me a great sense of achievement.

I'd been picking strawberries for about a week, and was walking home from the station, when a neighbour stopped me. It was Mrs Smith. She was at her door, and she asked me if Mam was home.

'I'm not sure,' I said.

'Well, if she is, could you ask her to call in?' I said I would.

Later that evening, I was playing with my brothers and sisters. By then there were six of us. We were playing in the big back bedroom. That's where I slept – sharing an iron hospital-type bed with Liz. Margaret slept in the room too, and the boys were sharing a single bed, next door in the box room.

I was putting a show on to keep the kids happy. I got dressed up and was pretending to be a singer. I don't have a note, but my brother John would pretend to have a guitar and we would be Sonny and Cher. Or John would be Elvis. The kids thought it was really funny. It made everyone laugh. John would burst out from behind a curtain that we put up between two presses, and sing 'All Shook Up'. The angels would always be with us laughing. It was nice when we had fun like that.

That night, there was a knock at the door. I shouted to Mam, 'I'll get it,' and I ran downstairs and opened the door. There at the door was Mr Smith.

'Hello, Mr Smith,' I said. 'Mam is in the kitchen, shall I get her for you?'

He nodded, then he came in and I closed the door. He went into the sitting room and sat down and I went to tell Mam Mr Smith was there. Then I went back upstairs to my brothers and sisters. I had only just got there when she shouted, 'Patricia!' I went out.

She said, 'Did you – or did you not – tell me Mr Smith was in the sitting room?'

'Yes.' I was puzzled. 'I did tell you. He is. I just let him in.'

'Patricia. That's just not funny. Will you stop messing.'

I couldn't think what she was going on about, but as she was giving out to me another knock came. Mam was right beside the door. She was still giving out to me as she opened it. It was Mrs Smith. She was crying.

'It's my husband,' she wailed. 'He's dead. He just died.' She could hardly get the words out, she was sobbing so much.

'When was this?'

'I just got a call from the hospital.'

I didn't understand. How could Mr Smith be dead, when he was sitting on our sofa as large as life? He was wearing normal clothes – black trousers with a shirt, a tie and a jumper. And his shoes were so shiny you could almost see your reflection in them. And it wasn't as if he was looking sick. There was colour in his cheeks. He looked absolutely fine to me. I assumed everyone could see him. So what was all the fuss about? Without thinking I said it.

'Don't be silly. He's not dead. There he is, sitting on the sofa.'

Mrs Smith was in tears and Mam said, 'Not again, Trisha. You have to stop this.'

'But he's here.' I'd hardly got the words out when she gave me a clatter – a right big slap.

She said, 'Wait until your dad comes home. He'll soon sort you.'

I was very upset. My angels were all around me. They explained that not everyone could see what I could.

'People won't always understand,' they said. 'And one day life, for you, will get much tougher because of what you can see.'

'But why did it happen? Why did Mr Smith come here, and how come I could see him, and nobody else could?'

'Mr Smith knew his wife would go to your mam when she heard the bad news. He'd want to be there, so he could see her one last time. It was his way of saying goodbye.'

'But if I'm going to get a clatter every time I see spirits, I won't have a head left.' I was laughing, though I didn't think it was all that funny. I was sitting on the bed holding my face where Mam had hit it. I was still listening to the angels when John came in.

'Are you in trouble, Trish?' I nodded. 'Would you like me to help you?'

There wasn't much he could do, but I thought it was nice that he'd asked. He was sensitive like me. He didn't like to see anyone hurting.

I sat him down and said, 'John, do you see angels?'

He looked at me with his face all screwed up. John had huge big eyes and lots of freckles. He looked so sweet and innocent. 'Angels? You mean like in books?'

'Yeah, a bit like that.'

'Why? Are angels real?'

I nodded. 'Yes, John. Everyone has a guardian angel. Your

angel is with you from the time you are born until the time you die and go to heaven. It will go to heaven with you.'

'Do our angels mind us?'

'Of course they do.'

'Then why can't I see my angel?'

'So you can't see angels?' I was disappointed then. I'd really thought that, maybe, John could. 'I really don't know.'

He looked thoughtful then. He said, 'If they mind us like you say, why are you always getting a clatter for talking to them?'

I just looked at his puzzled little face, and all I could do was laugh. But I tried to explain it all to him.

'You know we are very poor, and sometimes you, me and Mam go out for very long walks?'

'Yes.' He sighed then. 'Those walks are too long.'

'But the angels help us, because on those walks we go to get food, don't we? And aren't the nuns very good for giving us food?'

'Oh. You mean the nuns. You mean the nuns are angels?'

This was hard. 'Well, in a way they are. The nuns certainly help us. But that's not what I mean. The angels tell me that these people are kind and will give us food.' It was very hard trying to explain, so I gave up then. It was hard begging for food too. But getting even a bit always got us through.

I loved going to see Dad's parents, Nanny Bridget and Granddad Michael. I'd go and visit as much as I could. Granddad was a very strict man, but he was also understanding. I loved him, and loved going over to his house. He should have lived in the country really. Not in Ballyfermot. He had a vegetable patch in the garden. He loved digging and growing things. Nothing ever went to waste.

Granddad loved a joke too. He'd often read his newspaper upside down. He'd see how long it would take me to notice. That was his way. He could be really sensitive too, though. He'd notice if I was a bit sad.

Then he'd pat me on my head, and say, 'Let it out. Don't hold it in.'

And of course Nan could see the spirit world. So every time I would see a spirit, I could tell Nan, and she would say, 'Let them say what they need to say, and they can move on.'

I loved talking to Nan, because I never got into trouble over talking about angels or spirits. She fully understood.

Everyone called me the odd child. I was very much a loner. I found it hard to mix with people. It was almost like I didn't fit in. All the girls my age had really nice clothes and records. I didn't have that. It was simple. We couldn't afford it, so I never asked for things. People said I was wise beyond my years. And I was lucky, the angels were with me – they were my friends.

In May 1974, when I was almost thirteen, I went into town with Dad, and met Granddad Michael in town. It was a regular thing for us. Dad would sometimes take me in on a Friday. When we arrived, Dad would go straight to the pub. Granddad, though, wasn't a drinker. He'd have one glass of stout if he was out with my grandmother, but if she wasn't there, he wouldn't take a drink at all.

I loved meeting Granddad in town. He'd take me to a café in Talbot Street. That was his treat to me. He was a funny man. I never knew with him if he was being serious or if he was joking. He always wore a trilby hat and an overcoat, and his glasses would be on the end of his nose. For some reason, though, that day felt different. It had felt different from the time I got up. I was normally happy to be on the bus going to town, but that day I felt sad. I couldn't explain, even to myself, why that was.

Granddad noticed, though. He always did. He could see that I was disturbed in some way. He tapped me, very gently on my forehead, and said, 'Just let it go, Patricia. Just let it go. Whatever it is, just give it to me. I'll take your worries.'

I looked up at him and I smiled. And I said, 'Why do you always do that?'

And he said, 'Isn't it better that I take everything that is bothering you, so that it isn't bothering you any more?'

Granddad hated wasting anything. I used to order steak and chips, and I'd ask for two slices of bread to go with it. If I only ate one, as I often did, Granddad would always embarrass me. He'd ask for a brown paper bag, and he'd make me take the other slice of bread home.

I loved going around the shops with him. I adored just window shopping and he loved just walking around town. He'd usually have some errands too. Nan would give him a list.

After lunch, we looked in Guineys window as we were walking by. As we got to the second window, on the opposite side of the road, I noticed a child in a buggy. It looked as if it had been pushed away from its parents, who were standing there chatting. I remember thinking that was odd, because there was nobody there to do the pushing. The child's dad looked round in amazement.

We were going around the corner, when there was this big black cloud. A shiver went down my spine. I remember hearing something loud, but I wasn't sure what it was. Granddad was thrown to the ground. I was too. It was like we were blown off our feet. I remember there were bits of glass, afterwards, just fragments, on my cheek and my chin and my nose.

My hands were covered to. I was in a daze. I still couldn't be sure what had happened.

It was a while before I realized a bomb had gone off. That was something that just didn't happen in Dublin. It happened in Belfast — we all knew that — but not in Dublin.

Granddad picked me up. He said to me, 'Are you OK?'

I nodded. Looking back, I think I was lucky. I must have been pretty near the bomb that day. I remember I looked across the street and there was a car turned over on its roof. And there was a child, covered in black dust. She was lying on the road, absolutely still. I was pretty sure she was dead. I could see the angels all around.

There was such chaos. There were people running. People screaming. People crying. And people just lying there, blown to bits. And there was so much noise. There were sirens, alarms, horns. There was black smoke everywhere, and people were just running. Running, but not sure what direction they should go in. I could feel so much sadness. The angels were all around the people who were hurt. And those who had passed away.

I remember the dust. Dust everywhere. It got into my throat — into my eyes. My eyes were really sore. I could feel grit in the back of my eyes. I rubbed at them, but that only made it worse.

Granddad just wanted to get me to safety. That's all he kept saying. Meanwhile the gardaí had arrived on the scene. They were trying to get everyone to leave the street. There was a lot of confusion.

Then Granddad started worrying about my dad. He wanted to go and find him, but he didn't want me to go with him.

'Just get to safety, Patricia,' he said.

I wanted to go with him. I remember being in shock and crying.

The angels were there with me and they kept saying, 'Keep walking. Your dad is OK.'

So that's what I did. I went with everyone who was being ushered away, and we ended up at the train station. I will never forget being on that train. It was the loneliest journey. There were so many people on the train; it was full, but everyone was in shock. Nobody spoke. It was just silence. There was a sense of disbelief.

I remember looking down at my hands and seeing all these little fragments of glass. There was a man opposite me on the train and I could see the blood from his head running down his face. He was wearing a white shirt, and it was covered in blood. There was a woman sitting next to him. I remember she took a real handkerchief out of her bag, and tried to wipe away the blood.

As I watched, I thought about the baby I'd seen pushed to safety. And I thought, *That must've been the angels*. After a while, the train came to a complete halt. These soldiers boarded the train and started taking everyone off it. They said there'd been a bomb on the tracks. I don't remember exactly where that was, but I remember walking up a hill. I walked home then. It was so lonely. The angels were telling me that Granddad was OK, and that Dad was too, but I couldn't forget all that I'd seen. All those people who were hurt or blown apart.

When, finally, I got home, Mam burst into tears.

'Thank God you're all right,' she said. 'But look at you. Look at you.'

I went to the kitchen to look in the mirror that hung over the sink. It was as if someone had tipped a white grade powder all over me. I just cried and cried and cried.

'But where's your dad? Where's your granddad?'

I explained that Granddad had gone back to find Dad. And that first he'd directed me the way the gardaí wanted us all to walk. Then I told her about the train; about how it had stopped and how we'd all had to walk.

'Look at your face!' said Mam. She carefully washed off all the dust, and then, noticing all the splinters of glass, she went to fetch some tweezers, and carefully took them out. It hurt, but it was good that she did it. It made me feel cared for. I looked at her face as she gently cleaned the cuts, and I could see she was hurting. I thought, *She really loves me*. I'd never really thought that before.

Mam was in such a state though. She was so worried about Dad that she couldn't keep still. She kept going out of the front door and looking up the street. She kept doing that for hours and hours.

Dad finally got home at midnight. He had a couple of cuts on him. He had heard the blast from the pub, and the vibration had knocked him off his stool. But he'd thought it was someone just messing. He never spoke about all those hours before he got home. Never. But I think he was helping people who'd been hurt. I know if he'd seen someone hurt, he would help. For all his faults, Dad was good like that.

I thought about that day for a long time afterwards, but I never spoke about it again. I did ask the angels, 'Why did that happen? Why do people plant bombs and hurt other people? Why do they injure people and kill? And why can't you stop them?'

'Patricia, there is good and there is evil. All angels get very sad when bad things happen, but none of us is able to stop those bad things happening. What we can do is try and help people to stay in the light – the light they were born with. We try to stop people from getting into the power of evil. That is why it is so important that you speak to your angel every day. And Patricia – you should say a prayer, every day, asking for peace around the world.'

Some time later, we were all over with my grandparents on a visit, when Granddad Michael said to Mam, 'I'll take the bigger kids on a walk.'

When he said this my brother John looked at me and said, 'Does Granddad need some food?'

Poor Mam. Her face went really red.

Nan looked at us. I think she knew what had been going on, that Dad had been drinking the money, and that we'd had to go and get food from the nuns, but she wasn't about to embarrass Mam.

She just said, 'Go on now. Go and enjoy the walk. I'll have dinner ready for when you get back.'

It was her way of saying 'I know'. She was good to us. She always gave Mam a bag of food when it was time to go home. There was always fruit in that bag.

Anyway, me, Liz and John went with Granddad, and the little ones stayed with Mam and Nanny Bridget. Liz and John ran on ahead, and I stayed beside Granddad. He asked me if I was OK.

'Yes. Of course I am.' I smiled at him.

He didn't say anything more just then. And soon after he sat on a wall, and said it was break time. John and Liz ran back. We knew that in Granddad's paper bag there was a bottle of red lemonade. There'd also be an apple for each of us, and a sweet. They'd be those hard-boiled sweets and I could make one last forever.

As we sat there, the angels came and told me that Granddad was worried about me. And when we stood up to go back to his house, and John and Liz ran off again, he said it.

'Patricia, I'm worried about you.' I remember thinking, *This is great. I get to hear things before anyone actually says them.* The angels explained that that wasn't always the case.

'Patricia, we've never spoken about that bomb. How are you coping?'

I just looked at him, and shook my head. I couldn't talk about it. So he tapped me on the forehead, and told me he'd take over my worries.

'You should try and talk about it, Patricia. It was a terrible day. For me and your dad, as well as for you. It would help me, too, if you talk about it.' But I still kept quiet. 'Maybe I should have stayed with you.' I think he was talking to himself. 'Maybe I shouldn't have sent you off alone.' He sighed. 'I wish you would talk about that journey; about how you felt. If you don't it might just fester inside.'

I told him I'd felt lonely. And then I mentioned that the angels had helped me.

'Oh, speak to Nan,' he said. He hated it when I mentioned angels. The one thing I couldn't do, though, was to talk about the scene of the bomb. I could not bear to. Not then, and not for many years. I still find it difficult to talk about it today. The picture has stayed with me, always.

5 Sadness of Loss

If you respect the spirit world, the spirit
world will respect you.

When I was fourteen, I was working in a sewing factory in town. My dad was away at that time, working in England. As I left work, Archangel Michael said, 'Patricia, you must go straight home.'

I knew straight away that something was wrong, but I didn't want to think about it. I got on the bus for home, but as it pulled out my heart sank.

'I'm worried,' I said to the angels. 'I'm worried something bad is happening to me.' I was, too. I was terrified at the thought of my brothers and sisters managing without me.

'No, Patricia. You're going to be OK,' they said. But, even though I asked again, they wouldn't tell me what was wrong. Then the bus stopped and a man in a black coat and a trilby hat got on. That put me in mind of Granddad Michael – it was the way he dressed too. And I realized something bad must've happened to him. I started crying. And once I'd started I couldn't stop. Everyone on the bus was looking at me as if I was mad.

I was frightened to go home because I knew I'd hear bad news. It was like, if I don't go home, it won't be true. So I went to a friend's house instead. I'd known Rose for years and years. We'd always got on. We were chatting away together, telling each other news from the last couple of days. We were both mad about the Bay City Rollers. They'd just released 'Bye Bye Baby', and Rose had bought the record. She was playing it to me. Normally, I'd have been dancing around the room, but not that day. It was as much as I could do to listen to all her chat. That's because the angels kept interrupting. They kept telling me that I really must go home.

'Your mam is looking for you,' they said.

But I wouldn't listen. Rose had gone to her chest of drawers, and she pulled out her new three-quarter-length jeans. They had tartan going up the side.

'I'd love a pair of them,' I said, and she held them out to me.

'Try them on, Trish. See how they look.' I did, and I thought I looked like the bee's knees. I paraded around, admiring myself in the mirror.

'I'm definitely going to get a pair of these,' I said. Though, of course, I knew I never would. Where would I get the money for new clothes? Rose knew that too. She knew how things were for me.

'I've seen a pair I like better,' she said. 'The tartan is a different colour and I prefer them.' I'd taken the jeans off, and she was putting them back in the drawer. 'I'm trying to persuade Dad to give me the money for them. And when I get them, you can have these if you like.'

'Do you mean it?' I was excited at the thought.

The angels were around me still, but they weren't talking to me any more. It was as if they wanted me to have a bit of fun before I had to face what was to come. I told them, again, that I wasn't going home. And they looked at me with great sadness. They knew that my heart was heavy. They said that they'd look after me, always.

'You remember we spoke about heaven?' they said. And of course I remembered. It's a beautiful place with no pain, no arguments and no suffering.

'Why?' I asked. 'Am I going there?' I began to worry about myself again.

The angels laughed. 'Patricia. You're not going to heaven – at least, not yet.'

I was about to ask them, in that case, why they were talking about heaven, but at that moment a knock came on the door. It was my mam. She had tears in her eyes. She asked me why I'd not gone home. It was hard to answer. Hard to admit that I'd stayed away because I just knew that something was wrong.

'There is something wrong, isn't there?'

'How did you know, Trish?'

Without thinking, I said, 'The angels told me.' When I said that Mam gave me such a look. She raised her eyes, as if to say, 'Not again.'

'Patricia, let's go.' She reached for my hand, but I pulled away. I really thought that if I stayed, nobody could give me bad news. But the angels stepped in. They reminded me they were there for me and persuaded me to go.

Mam was quiet as we walked home. It was as if she didn't know what way to give me the bad news. When we got home my dad's sister was there with her husband.

That's when Mam said, 'Patricia, Granddad Michael died today.'

Even though I knew it was something like that, I couldn't take it in. I put my hands over my ears.

I said, 'I can't hear you.'

I couldn't understand how he could leave this life without telling me. He was a strong man, and he was full of wisdom.

'He can't be dead. He wasn't even sick.' I started crying and the angels came into the room.

'Is this really true?' I asked them. 'Is Granddad really in heaven?'

'Yes, Patricia, it is.'

'But why? Why did you take him? Why could he not stay?'

'It was his time.'

My aunt Margaret and her husband, John, took me over to see Nan. When we arrived Nan took me to one side.

'Your granddad is happy and at peace,' she said. 'And you're not to worry. You still have me.' She smiled, and gave me a big hug. 'And while I'm here, you are safe.'

She meant that I was safe talking about the angels. And that she believed me when I talked about the spirit world.

She'd always say, 'If you respect the spirit world, the spirit world will respect you.' She knew my love for the angels was strong. She'd always known that. When people would call me a strange child, Nan would always say, 'No. Patricia is special.'

I liked that, even though I never saw myself as special. For me, seeing the spirit world was just normal.

The day we went to the funeral home to say goodbye to Granddad, everyone was upset. I went in to see the coffin, but I froze. I stood back from the coffin, too afraid to go nearer.

Nan took me by the hand and said, 'It's OK. I'll stand with you.'

We walked up and I looked at Granddad. He didn't look dead. He looked exactly as he had the last time I'd seen him. I bent over him and gave him a kiss. Then I looked up, and saw Granddad standing at Nan's side. There were two angels standing beside him. I told this to Nan. She smiled.

'I told you he was OK,' she said. 'He's happy. He's in heaven and that's a happy place.'

'I know that,' I said. 'The angels told me, but why does my heart hurt?'

Nan explained that hurting was normal; that everyone who lost someone felt like that.

'But you're lucky,' she said. 'You can see into heaven and know what it's like.'

On the day of the funeral, I decided to walk behind the coffin rather than go in a funeral car. His sons and daughters did the same. As we walked, Granddad walked beside me. I looked around to see if my aunts and uncles could see him, and I knew by their faces that they couldn't. That excited me. I felt so tall walking with him.

'Will I see you again?' I asked him.

'I will always watch over you,' he said. 'And remember, Patricia, always walk tall.'

When we walked into the church there were angels everywhere. It was beautiful. I felt like shouting it out, but I stopped myself. I knew I'd only get into trouble. So I got on with the day. We all went back to Nan's house after the service. I stayed there with Nan for a few days.

I felt so sad. When I stayed in their house in Ballyfermot, I stayed in their bedroom. They had a double bed, but they also had a single bed in there. They kept that especially for me. There was a statue of the sacred heart at the end of my bed. It had a red light on it. Granddad had always figured it was going to protect me.

I'd loved being there and talking to Granddad. He used to say I would never shut up! I'd help him with his vegetables. I remember he had amazing rhubarb too. I was always interested in that.

Nan just loved writing. She had a bureau in the front room, and she'd sit there writing away. She had beautiful handwriting.

Normally, when I was staying in Ballyfermot, there'd be lots of sing-songs. Nan was musical. She played the piano and the accordion, and she was great at singing too. I remember she taught me to sing 'Four Green Fields'. I used to love drumming. I'd put the pots all out, and drum on them. Nan always told me I had a good sense of rhythm.

The week after Granddad died, though, there was no music. Nan and I just wanted to be together. I don't know if I was comforting her, or if she was comforting me, but it was good just to be in the house with her.

I couldn't stay too long, though. I had to get home. I knew my brothers and sisters needed me. Without me there wasn't enough money, and they'd have nothing.

When I was fifteen Nan became ill. She never made a fuss, and it took a lot of coaxing to get her to hospital. She was having tests done, but I knew, in my heart, that this was serious. And it was. The doctors found a tumour on her leg, and they had to amputate it. I was horrified. But Nan didn't want a fuss.

She was a really determined lady. I think it's where I get my determination from. When she had her leg amputated, she still walked home. She wouldn't come out in the wheelchair.

She said, 'I walked into the hospital. And I'm going to walk out.'

And she did. She used a frame, but she walked.

From then on she just got on with it. When she first got home, I remember saying to her, 'What are you going to do, Nan, with just one leg?'

Nan nearly fell down laughing.

'Patricia, what am I going to do with you?' I was crying. 'You don't need to cry. I'll get around perfectly with one leg.' And she did. Nothing stopped Nanny Bridget.

It was as she said: 'If you tell yourself you can't, then you won't.'

A year later I noticed Nan was in pain. And she wasn't getting around as well as she had done. I asked the angels to help her. This bright green light came into the room. And beside Nan stood this wonderful angel. He said he was Raphael, and that he was the angel of healing. I felt relieved.

'Are you going to heal my nan?'

'No. I can't do that, but I can ease her pain.' He told me that soon she would join my grandfather in heaven, but in the meantime he would stay around her to help.

'Patricia, are you seeing something?' Nan was looking at me intently.

'You always know, don't you?' I said. 'How do you know when I see things?' She looked at me with her gentle eyes, and took my hand in both of hers. My heart was breaking to see her looking so frail.

'I can see it in your face,' she said. 'It changes a little and your eyes stay very still. I know, then, that you are talking to angels.'

I decided then that I'd be more careful. I was so afraid that other people would notice, as she had, and that they would think I was mad.

'Patricia.'

'Yes, Nan.'

'Don't ever doubt what God gave you. Don't ever think it's your imagination.' She looked at me so intently. 'And, Patricia, never let anyone tell you that you're mad. Promise me now.'

I thought this was such a strange thing for her to say. I wondered if it was the tablets making her say silly things. And all the while I was practising keeping my face normal, while the angels were talking to me at the same time as Nan was. I wasn't successful. Nan said my face looked really funny, and then we both had a good laugh. And a good cry too. I think that was the best healing for both of us.

'Nan, can you feel it when the angels are around? Did you see the Angel Raphael? He was here earlier to help you with your pain. He said he can't heal you, but he can make things better. He was so beautiful. Did you sense him?'

'Yes, I always know. And I know I'll soon be going to heaven.'

I told her I knew that too. I said the angels had told me.

'You must always listen to the angels,' she said. 'They'll look after you when I'm gone.'

Nan was alive for a few months more. She was frail, and spent a lot of time sleeping. But in between we'd have our little chats. I saw her as much as I could. I'd go to Mam's house straight after work, then I'd go on to Nan's house. And when she got weaker, I'd go straight to Nan's house. I wanted to be with her at the end.

One day I had a message to go to Mam's house. She needed me. I worried about Mam. She was pregnant with her ninth child, and I hadn't been home much over the past months. My brothers and sisters were really happy to see me. So was Mam.

'Is there something wrong?' I asked. 'Why did you send for me?'

'I need your help with the kids,' she said.

'But Nan is very sick. She needs me there.'

'Patricia, there are loads of people looking after your nan. There is no need for you to be there as well.'

I stood there in shock. The house was in a state. The fire wasn't lit, and it looked as if the place hadn't been cleaned since I'd last been there. I started crying. I knew Nan would die soon, and I couldn't stop. Mam asked me why I was crying. I looked at her, sure that she knew. I loved my mam. But sometimes I wished she would give me a hug and tell me everything was going to be OK. But she never did.

I ran off then. I knew in my heart this was Nan's last day. The bus was just leaving, but I shouted and it stopped for me. When I arrived, I ran into Nan's house. Everyone was in the front room where she was.

As I stepped in my aunt Lily said, 'Patricia, she's gone.' I couldn't believe it. I'd felt sure she would wait for me. They said she hadn't wanted me to see her die. But that she'd waited until she heard me come into the house before she closed her eyes and died.

'We'll leave you here with your nan,' said my aunt. 'You can say goodbye to her in peace.'

I sat on the bed. Nan was propped up. She was still warm. I had a chat to her as if she was still alive.

'Why did you die just then, Nan?' I asked. 'Why didn't you wait for me? You were supposed to wait for me.' I started to cry. 'I'm really going to miss you. I wish you could live forever.' I was holding her hand, telling her how much I loved her, when all of a sudden her head came forward and she belched. I got such a shock. I thought, *They've made a mistake. She's not dead.* I ran out to tell them so.

They were all drinking tea in the kitchen, and sorting things out for the funeral.

'Stop all that,' I said. 'Nan's not dead. I tell you, she's not. It's a mistake. She just sat up and belched.' They all burst out laughing. I couldn't believe it. One aunt took me back into the front room. I expected Nan to be talking and breathing, but she wasn't.

I took her hand and said, 'Talk, Nan. Show them you're alive.'

I explained to my aunt, again, about the belch.

'Patricia, that sometimes happens,' she said. 'It was just a bit of wind being released. Not a sign of life.' Then she started to laugh again.

'It wasn't funny!'

'No,' she said. 'But the look on your face was.'

Now, when I look back on it, I can see the funny side; now I really do laugh.

After that, I sat there, still talking to Nan. I felt a great sense of calmness. That room became full of light. I knew the angels were all around there, and in my mind's eye I could see Nan really happy. She was happy to see Granddad. I felt lonely, but I knew Nan would help me from heaven. I knew that. My heart was broken, but I knew she wasn't in pain any more. I knew, too, that she was a very much loved woman.

We got everything ready for her funeral, and we got through that day. As at Granddad's funeral, there were lots of angels around and that really helped me to get through. That night, though, as I was saying my prayers, I was worrying about what I would do now that Nan had gone. Who would I talk to about the spirit world and the angels?

When I opened my eyes I saw Nan standing next to Granddad. They looked so happy and healthy. Then Nan reminded me that I mustn't forget about the angels.

'They will help you,' she said. 'You must never forget that or doubt them. But you are going to have to be strong. God gave you your gifts so that you can help the people around you, but there will be people who won't believe that they are there.' Then she repeated her earlier warning. She said, 'People may try and tell you that you're mad. Don't let them.'

Then a beautiful white light came, and Nan and Granddad disappeared. This was March 1979.

6 Meeting My Spirit Guide

My spirit guide helps the spirit world connect, and
makes sure that only the truth is spoken.

By this time I was working in Dublin, in a small factory
making clothes. It was a lovely place to work, almost like a
little family. I never had new clothes; my clothes always came
in a big bag from St Vincent de Paul, but I never looked too
out of place. I'd have one skirt which I would wash over and
over again. After a while it would look a bit worn, but not so
much that people noticed. It never bothered me.

Some of the other girls looked really nice. They could
keep most of their wages, and could buy themselves some
lovely clothes. Of course I always admired them. But I didn't
waste time envying them, or thinking, *Why can't I have that?* I
think I just accepted it.

The boss at the factory was very fair, and we all got on
well. On Fridays, all the girls would go to a pub straight from
work. They asked me to go with them, and sometimes I did.
I'd have a lemonade – I didn't want to drink alcohol. I was
frightened of drinking, because I could see what it did to
Dad. One week, all the girls were going dancing after the
pub. They asked me to go with them, but I made my excuses.
I said, 'Maybe another time.'

I'd have loved to have gone; the girls were all so nice, but
I couldn't afford it. I had to buy food for the family, and there

were bills to pay. We were all having a great laugh. They were talking about all the things they did on weekends out. It sounded like they had so much fun.

Then this girl came in who I'd never seen before. Her name was Paula. She was chatty and bubbly. We were getting on really well when I said, 'I can see a spirit man behind you. Oops.'

I immediately put my hand up in front of my mouth – as if I could push the words back again. I hadn't meant to say it out loud; I was in shock, because I'd never said something like that in public before. The angels made me happy; they were my friends, but I never told anyone about them. How could I? The poor girl looked shattered. She looked at me as if I was completely mad.

'I'm so sorry,' I said. 'I didn't mean to frighten you.'

By now the Archangel Michael was standing beside the spirit man. He told me that the spirit was the girl's father. He wanted his daughter to know that he was OK and happy. I thought, *Here I am in a pub on a Friday night, talking to the angels.* It was strange. How could I possibly pass on the message without sounding mad? I turned to Paula.

'Listen. I promise you, I'm not mad, but sometimes I see people who have died.'

She looked at me as if to say 'Right!'

I told her that her dad was in the spirit world and wanted her to know he was happy.

'Ah,' she said. 'I get it now. One of the girls must have told you my dad had died.'

'No.' Why would she think that? Nobody had ever even mentioned Paula's name. 'They didn't. Honest. Look, will you come somewhere quieter? Then I can ask your dad to tell you something personal.'

'But, Patricia, I don't believe in all that stuff.' She sighed deeply. But she followed me out of the pub. My heart was pounding. I thought I was going to get into trouble again. I muttered to her dad that he'd better have something good to say for all the trouble he was putting me through. I know that sounds harsh. But I said it with a smile. I'd discovered by then that the spirit world can have a great sense of humour.

Spirits would say, 'Just because we're not on earth doesn't mean we can't laugh.'

I became aware of a tall black man. 'What are you doing here?' I asked.

'Trust me,' he said. 'I'm your guide, here to help you with the spirit world.' I couldn't stop laughing. 'You'll get to know me in time.'

The angels were telling me to control myself. 'You have a job here, Patricia,' they said. 'You must listen and pass on whatever message you get.'

So I calmed down and turned to the girl's father. I could see he was a hard-working, loving man. He told me a story about the girl when she was young. I passed that on. But she wasn't convinced.

'That's pot luck,' she said.

The angels were standing by her side. They said, 'Be patient with her. She's hurting. She misses her father very much.' I turned to her spirit father and asked him to tell me more.

'Tell her I'm sorry.' He was getting upset. It made me want to cry, but I passed on the message.

'Is he saying *why* he is sorry?' Paula asked.

'Tell her I was weak at that moment. Tell her if I'd known the hurt and pain my death would cause I would never have done it.' Then he said, 'Ask her why she never reads the letter I left for her.'

When I asked her that she just burst into tears. 'I couldn't read it,' she said, sobbing. 'If I read the letter, it would make his death real. I'm just living day by day, and it's hard.'

It turned out that he had taken his own life, and the girl had convinced herself it was all her fault. I then thanked God and the angels for allowing me to pass on that message. It meant that the girl was able to finally heal.

I left the pub after that, and took a bus home. I felt really tired and I asked the angels what was wrong with me.

'You need to rest. Giving such a long message will take a lot out of you.' They were right. It had.

When I got off the bus, I decided to get some chips because the kids at home loved them. After I'd ordered them I went out for a smoke and my spirit guide was there. I said, 'Oh, go away, won't you? I'm tired.' I'd been speaking out loud. It was hard not to. He was so real to me, I forgot that other people couldn't see him. I'm sure they all thought I was mad. I must've looked hilarious. As the guide is tall and I'm five foot one, I was looking up at him. I had my back to the chipper and there I was chatting away.

He smiled. 'I'm here to stay. And look,' he pointed at the chipper. 'Your chips are ready.'

I said, 'How do you know my chips are ready?' I turned round. He was right. The girl was waving at me through the window, and everybody in the queue was staring at me. I felt really stupid.

'You made a right fool out of me,' I said to him when I'd got my chips.

'No. You made a fool of yourself,' he said. 'You were the one talking out loud. You shouldn't do that. You have to learn to trust me. I've always been with you. Whether you want me to or not, I'm staying.'

'OK. If you're my so-called guide, what exactly do you do?'

'I help the spirit world connect, and make sure that only the truth is spoken.'

'Have you a name?'

'I'm Andrew.' So there I was walking up the road talking to Andrew, quite forgetting that I was the only person who could see him. We were having a great chat. So much so that when I got home, I didn't notice Dad on his way out until he shouted at me.

'Patricia! You're talking to yourself. Again. You do know that's the first sign of madness?' I hated it when he put me down like that. But he didn't say anything else. He just set off for the pub. The rest of us had a great, relaxed night. We ate the chips with bread and butter and talked about anything and everything. It really warmed my heart to see the kids so happy. To see them play and not get into trouble for it. John was twelve by then.

He said, 'Why can't it be like this all the time?' He loved it that, with Dad out, there was nobody going on about the noise.

'You mustn't hate Dad,' I said. 'I'm sure there's a reason he's the way he is.' He didn't look convinced.

'Why don't you ask those angels of yours to send Dad away? Then we can all be happy, always.' He paused. 'And if they won't I'll do my karate chops on him.' I laughed as John showed me all the new moves he'd learned. He was pulling all these faces in concentration. It made me fall around laughing. That didn't please John.

'It's not funny.' I just hugged him then, and tried to explain I was laughing because I was happy. But he was in a mood with me. He pulled away.

'I'm not talking to you, Yaya.' He began to throw himself

around in a temper. I was about to calm him down when Andrew burst into the room. He seemed so out of place there. He's so tall, and is as black as the ace of spades.

'What do you want now?' I asked Andrew. 'Can't you see I'm busy?' John looked startled. But it stopped his temper stone dead. 'Sorry,' I said to John. 'I was talking to someone else.'

I felt silly. Andrew's presence was completely different from the other angels. When they came they would send out so much light; and they'd be gentle. Andrew arrived with a bang, and I wasn't used to it. I was trying to calm John down and talk to Andrew, and that must have looked really strange to John. He was used to me talking to the angels but this was like an outburst. He gave me an odd look and went running into the sitting room to my mam.

'Mam! She's at it again. Patricia's talking to spirits again!'

I looked at Andrew and said, 'That's it! You're going to have to stop this. I get into enough trouble for talking to angels.'

I went out and sat on the stairs. I felt really sorry for myself. I was thinking, *What am I going to do?*

I wished my Nan was there. I thought, *She would know exactly what to do.* As soon as I'd thought that, I felt this comforting heat on my hand. I tried to see what it was but I couldn't. I could only feel it.

Mam came out then. She wasn't happy. 'Patricia, this has to stop.'

'But, Mam. It's not my fault that I see dead people. I don't ask them to talk to me.'

'Well, tell them you're not allowed to talk to them any more.'

That upset me more. I went to bed feeling really tired. I

got ready for bed, then said my prayers. I asked God and the angels to help me to do the right thing. I didn't want my mam to get upset. Andrew appeared then.

I sighed. 'Oh, go away,' I said. 'Look at the trouble you've got me into.'

I got into bed then and turned over in a huff. I felt this tap on my shoulder. I ignored it, feeling sorry for myself. Then I felt the tap again. I jumped out of bed, furious. 'Is there something wrong with your hearing? I'm not talking to you.'

Andrew laughed. 'Are you finished?' I had to laugh then, and say I was sorry. He explained that he wasn't going away, that his job was to help the spirit world talk to me in the best way – without all talking at once.

'I can't make you communicate with them,' he said. 'It's up to you, but if you decide to listen to me, I will help you.' Then he told me that the heat I'd felt had been my Nan come to comfort me.

'Why couldn't I see her, when I can see everyone else?'

'Oh, Yaya. I know you've only seen her once since she passed away. You will see her again. Just give her time.'

'How do you know I'm called Yaya?'

'Oh!' He smiled. 'I know everything. But you need to rest now,' he said and he stood up. Then the angels came in. I could feel their warmth. It felt as if they were tucking me in. I fell fast asleep.

I woke, some hours later, with a start. I could hear Dad downstairs. He was shouting but I couldn't hear his words. I didn't get up. And eventually I fell back asleep again.

7 Struggling

The angels will never leave you. They will always be
by your side.

Nothing at home had really changed. I still had to get up at
six every morning. I'd clean and light the fire and sort out
the kids for school. Then I'd head out to work. Some days
I hadn't money for my bus fare, so I'd have to walk. That
meant I had to leave earlier. I didn't mind walking, but I
was just so tired by the end of the day. I'd finish work, get
home late in the evening, and have to help Mam with the
bottles and nappies. My poor mam. She'd just sit in a chair.
She didn't move out of that chair much at all, but you got
used to it. She'd no energy at all after having all those babies.
And the miscarriages. And the beatings. It took everything
out of her.

One Monday morning I was especially tired. I had to drag
myself out of bed.

I said to the angels, 'What is wrong with me? Can you help
me?'

'Go to the doctor,' they said. 'You really must.'

But I couldn't. I couldn't afford to take a day off work.

'You're suffering from exhaustion, Patricia,' they said. 'And
if you don't do something about it you'll end up getting
really ill.'

All I knew was that I was so tired. Tired all the time. I just wanted to sleep. But I couldn't take a day off work. Mam depended on my wages coming in. The angels kept on warning me. They said something strange.

They said, 'Remember we will never leave you. We'll be always by your side. Always and forever.'

I was puzzled. 'Why would I think you're going to leave me? I know you'll always be there with me.'

I got myself ready for work somehow, but I'd never felt so tired. I remember getting as far as the gate. Then I woke up on the sofa. Mam was there, and the smaller children too.

'What happened?' I asked. 'Why am I not at work?'

'You fainted,' said Mam. 'You collapsed at the gate.' That was a terrible shock. Nothing like that had ever happened to me before.

That was the start of it all. I went to the doctor after that. I had to. He told me I was suffering from stress and would have to slow down.

'You have a hard life, Patricia. But you can't go on carrying the load for your family. I know you feel you should, but you just don't have the strength.' My doctor knew me well. He knew that Dad was an alcoholic, who had a bad temper. He knew that Mam got tired and needed my help, and he knew there were lots of small children to care for. He knew all that.

'Patricia, you must rest,' said the doctor. 'You must rest as much as you possibly can.'

But I couldn't. I went straight back to work. I had no choice. Mam needed my wages, and my help with the kids. But I began to get worse. I would jump at every little sound, and I found the pressure of looking after my brothers and sisters became too much for me.

I was grieving too. I couldn't believe how much I missed Nanny Bridget. She was my guide. She was like my mother really. I always felt safe around my nan. She was the only one, really, who cared how I was. And of course she understood about the angels. I could say to her, 'I've seen the angels and the spirit world,' and she would nod, and understand. With her gone, nobody else ever did.

One night I was in the sitting room with Mam, trying to relax after a hard day at work. Dad came home in the worst mood ever. He'd run out of money for drink and he wasn't happy at all. I was so tired too. And though I heard my angels I couldn't see them. That really upset me. I burst into tears. And once I'd started crying, I couldn't stop.

I don't remember much about that evening. It's a blur to me. I remember the doctor calling to the house. I remember him saying to my dad it would be best if I went into the hospital for a while. I can remember being in the hospital, but how I got there is a blur.

I know that Dad took me into the hospital on the bus. I was upset still. I was crying and confused, and just so, so tired. I knew I was going in to see another doctor, because I'd heard the GP say so. They took me to Jervis Street Hospital, to a ward on the very top floor.

My first days in the hospital are a blur too. I remember the ward. It was really, really long. There was a big long table in the middle and there'd be three or four nurses sitting there. They'd be watching us, and filling in charts. The ward was part of an ordinary hospital, but we were very cut off there. I didn't even have visitors.

I remember they gave me an injection and it made me sleep. I slept for a good few days. There were about fifteen beds in that ward. I remember the other patients as old people, but they might have been in their forties or fifties — to me, at seventeen, that seemed old. I remember they kind of shuffled along. Nobody seemed to walk properly. Nobody had any energy. Some of the patients seemed very bad.

It felt very strange in hospital. They kept giving me all these pills to keep me woozy. I slept, on and off, for about ten days. During that time I could hear my angels but not see them clearly. But when I really woke, my head felt clearer. I felt better, and I felt the angels were close to me again. That made me so happy. I felt I was ready, now, to go home. And then, one day, a nurse said that the doctors wanted to see me.

'Just to see how you're getting on,' she said, and she led me out of the ward door, down this long, long corridor, to a room.

She knocked on the door, and this deep voice said, 'Come in.'

Opening the door, she said, 'I've brought you Patricia . . . come on in, Patricia.'

'Ah, yes.' The doctor looked up from the notes he was reading, leant forward and shook my hand. He smiled at me and said, 'How are you doing?'

'I'm doing just fine,' I said. 'And I'd really like to go home.'

He bent his head, and went back to the notes he'd been reading when I arrived. And I realized it was my chart. He seemed to be reading it for an awful long time. I remember sitting there fidgeting in the silence. Then he looked up at me and smiled. I remember thinking, *Isn't he nice?* All because he smiled a lot. And he had kind eyes.

Then he said to me, 'Do you ever feel you want to harm yourself?'

I jumped in shock. That was the last thing I'd expected him to say. 'God, no! Why would I want to do that?'

He seemed quite surprised by my answer. Then he said, 'Do you hear voices?'

'Not exactly voices. But I hear angels. Well, I see them too.

75

I couldn't when I first came in. I felt at one time that they'd left me. But now they're back again. That's because I'm now better.' I looked at him and he was smiling at me still, and nodding. 'Why? Do you hear angels too?'

When I said that, he gave me a very strange look. I thought, *Why is he looking at me like that?* Then my angels came into the room, and they told me not to say any more. But it was too late. The doctor was already interested in what I had said.

'Tell me more about the angels,' he said. I thought, *At last, someone else who believes in angels.* I told him how I had always seen angels and the spirit world, and how they would tell me things about people. And that when I was being abused, which was very difficult for me at that time, how the angels had stopped some of the pain, and how they gave me strength and helped me to be strong. I felt that the doctor was being very kind to me. I felt he really understood.

But then he looked at me and he said, 'Ah well, Patricia. We will soon stop those angels from telling you stupid things.'

I protested. I said, 'No, no. I don't want my angels to go away. I love them and they love me. They're my friends. I rely on them.'

That made it worse. The more I tried to tell him about the angels, the more he looked at me strangely. Then I made my biggest mistake.

'The angels are here with us right now,' I said. 'They're everywhere here.'

I know now what a mistake that was. I realize it must have made me seem mad. And certainly the doctor lost all patience with me. Shutting my chart with a bang, he sighed, and stood up to dismiss me.

'No, really! You must believe me. My angels protect me. They tell me things. They've given me messages for people.'

It was no good. He wasn't listening. I was still protesting. Still trying to get him to listen to me, and to understand, but of course he didn't. And just then two nurses came in to collect me again. One was the nurse who had brought me down. She was so nice.

'OK, Patricia. It's back to the ward now.'

'But I want to go home. I'm better. Really I am.' Why wouldn't they listen to me?

All they kept saying, as we were walking back to the ward, was, 'Patricia, don't worry. You will be going home very soon. But first you'll have to let the doctors make you better.'

When we got back to the ward they gave me an injection. I really don't remember a lot after that. I think I was asleep for a couple of days. After that I started coming round, but I was a bit woozy and I didn't understand what was going on with me. I was told I was going to go home after I'd had some other treatment. I said that was fine. I would have done anything to get out of there.

They said the treatment they were trying was called Electroconvulsive Therapy – ECT. I don't remember much about it. They took me into one of the small consulting rooms and gave me an injection. That made me more woozy, but I didn't go to sleep. There were two doctors with me, and there was a nurse there too. I remember them putting some wires on my head, and it looked like a hat. There were wires on my chest too – but I think those were there to check my heart rate. I'm not sure what the treatment was meant to do. I remember I felt sick after it. I didn't tell them that. I said I was great. I'd have said anything to get out of that place.

They asked me was I still hearing the voices or seeing angels, and inside my heart was breaking. I knew I was going to have to lie, because, yes, I was still seeing them. They were giving me comfort.

'No,' I told them. 'The voices have gone now.'

'That's great, Patricia,' they said. 'That means the treatment has worked.'

It was terrible in that hospital. They watched you every minute. And in that long ward, there was nowhere to go to be alone. Now that I was feeling more myself I began to explore. I'd walk down the corridor, past three rooms – the doctors' offices. At the end of the corridor there were two doors. Once, I walked along the corridor and tried to get through one of the doors. I thought that on the other side of the door I'd find reality. But it wouldn't open. When I pushed it really hard, I found that it was locked. It gave me a terrible shock.

A nurse came along and said the door was kept locked all the time. I asked her could she let me through, and she said, 'No, Patricia. You're not allowed through there.'

'Why not?'

'Because you're not ready to go home.'

After that, I became focused on the idea of getting home. I thought of nothing else. When the doctors asked about hearing voices or seeing angels I kept on lying.

I said, 'I don't see them any more.'

It really hurt me to lie to the doctors. I know that when I had the breakdown the doctors were telling me the angels were all in my imagination. I knew the only way I would ever get out of hospital would be to lie, and to say I wasn't seeing the angels any more. But I felt so sad that I had to do that. It broke my heart. My angels told me it was OK to lie. But to me, it wasn't. It was wrong. I was denying them.

When, finally, the doctors let me out of hospital, they gave me some tablets to take home. They said I must take the tablets every day.

'And you're to see a psychiatrist every month, to check how you are.' That sounded OK to me. Like I said, I would have done anything. And it really felt great to get out of that place. It really did.

8 Violent Times

The angels can't change your free will. But they will
always be there to help you.

I was good at following the doctors' orders. I was taking the
tablets, just like they had told me to do. I didn't dare do
anything else, but I didn't like taking them because they made
me feel so sleepy. It was like thinking through cotton wool.
After a couple of weeks, though, my body must've got used
to them.

About a month later I woke to hear the kids sneaking
downstairs, trying their best to be quiet. They knew better
than to wake Dad and tried to avoid the creaking stairs. They
rarely managed it. I got up feeling good, and went down to
the kitchen to get the kids some breakfast. I could hear them
in the sitting room. They were making way too much noise,
so I went in to tell them to be quiet.

There was a man asleep on the sofa. I recognized him as a
man who'd gone out drinking with Dad the night before. I'll
call him Barry here, though that is not his real name. He
woke just then, and looked amazed to see all these little faces
peering at him. He sat up, and put his hands on his head, as
if it hurt. I offered him some tea. He said, 'Thanks. I'd love
some,' and he smiled. After he'd drunk it he left, and I went
on with my day.

That night, Dad was going out again. And once again he

had Barry with him. From then on Barry was in and out of the house a lot. He and Dad seemed to have become best mates. Dad was a lot older than Barry. Dad was well into his thirties by then, and Barry was twenty-one. But anyone who enjoyed going out drinking was a friend of Dad's. It didn't matter how old or young they were.

I quite liked having Barry about the place, but then, one night, he asked me out. I was really surprised, I'd never been out with a boy.

'Oh, I don't know,' I said. But he didn't take that as an answer. He was very persistent. He asked me again, and then, when I still wouldn't give him an answer, he said it to Dad. For some reason, Dad was very happy at the idea. So in the end I gave in and agreed to go out with Barry. I remember he took me to the Concorde pub. That was our local.

And actually, he was great. He was very kind to me, and thoughtful. I liked that, and I liked that he kept himself very clean and tidy. I was impressed with him. We went out for a couple of months and things were going really well.

Then Dad fell out with Barry. I think, looking back, it was that he didn't like Barry being with me all the time, instead of him. Anyway, Dad threw me out of the house. I didn't know what to do.

That wasn't the first time it had happened. Dad would often go off in a temper and throw me out, even though I'd done nothing wrong. But before, I always had Nanny Bridget to go to, and of course she wasn't around any more.

Barry had a flat and he persuaded me to move in with him. All this time, though, Andrew, my spirit guide, had been warning me about Barry.

He said, 'Be careful. Barry is not a good person. He can be possessive, and violent too.'

'That's not true. Barry has shown me nothing but kindness. He's never even lost his temper.'

I thought it was love. I really did. I thought what the angels were saying was nonsense, because Barry *was* so kind. I suppose he gave me the love I craved from my dad. He was like my dad in the sense that he was militarized. He presented himself very well and I liked it that he was a good bit older than me. I was just eighteen.

I'll never forget the day I moved in with Barry. I was really happy and excited. But when we arrived at the front door, my guide Andrew and the Archangel Michael were standing there, blocking my way, telling me on no account to go in.

'Listen to us, Patricia,' they said. 'If you move in with Barry, you'll have a really tough time. Please don't do it.'

'You're wrong,' I said. 'Barry is good. I love him, and I want to live with him. Besides, you can't stop me.'

'We can't,' they agreed. 'We can't change your free will. And if you insist on moving in, we'll just have to stand by and let you. But we won't go away. We will always be here to help you.'

'Oh, fine,' I said. But I wasn't really listening. I really wanted to move in with Barry, and that was that. I felt sure everything would be OK. Why wouldn't it?

And at first, it was. The first week was heaven. Barry worked as a doorman at a nightclub. He was wonderful around the house, at keeping everything clean and tidy. I found that amazing. He was good to me too. There was nothing he wouldn't do for me. One of his friends called one night and asked us to a party. I thought that was great. I decided I'd buy myself a dress for the party. I was so excited, as I'd never bought anything for myself before. Well, I couldn't; I'd never had the money.

I hadn't abandoned my family now that I'd moved out. Dad would make sure I still sent money home. He'd come up and meet me each Friday, and I still handed money over. But now I was keeping some back. I felt guilty about that, but I had to live. There were things I needed. Even so, I wouldn't have done it, but the girls at work insisted that I should. They said that giving it all away wasn't right.

It wasn't that they all came from wonderful homes. One girl had a father who was an alcoholic too. But he didn't carry on in the same way that my dad did. Anyway, a girl from work offered to come shopping with me during our lunch break, to pick something out.

The first few dresses I tried weren't that great on me. But then I found one I really liked. It was black and white with a butterfly belt. I thought it was beautiful. And when I went out of the cubicle to do a twirl, my friend gasped.

'That's the one,' she said.

I felt so important. It was the first time in my life I ever had anything new. It made such a change from all those hand-me-downs. My friend said patent stilettos and a black bag would look good with it, but I hadn't any, and knew I'd not be able to afford any for a couple of weeks.

My friend said, 'Cinders, you will go to the ball!' We were both messing and laughing.

I couldn't wait for five o'clock to come so that I could get home and show Barry the dress. On the bus I kept peeking at my dress inside the bag, and smiling to myself. I could see the angels smiling too.

I said to them, 'Isn't life just great!'

'You might think so, Patricia. But Barry is not the man for you.'

I put my hands over my ears. I just didn't want to hear that.

Not when things were, at last, starting to go well for me. I just told myself that the angels had got it all wrong.

When I got home Barry was in. He hadn't any work that night.

'Hi, Patricia,' he said. 'You look happy. How was your day?'

'Oh, Barry! It was such fun. I went shopping at lunchtime. Look what I've bought.' I was so excited as I took my new dress out of its bag. 'What do you think?'

I expected him to be happy for me, and to admire the dress. I waited for him to smile, and maybe ask me to try the dress on for him, but a strange look came on his face.

He snatched the dress from me and shouted, 'What's this?'

I was in shock. I said, 'It's my new dress for the party of course.'

'New dress? But you didn't ask me if you could buy a dress.' He was really shouting.

'It's my money,' I said. 'I work hard for it and I can do what I like with it.' Before all my words were out, he punched me in the face. I was so shocked. I thought, *That didn't just happen.* He grabbed me then, and gave me a hug.

'I'm so sorry, Patricia,' he said. 'I don't know what came over me. I don't know why I punched you. Will you forgive me?'

And I did. Of course I did. But I couldn't go into work for the rest of the week. How could I when I had a black eye? I didn't go to the party either. Barry went without me, but, to be fair, he didn't stay very long. Meanwhile, the angels pleaded with me to leave him.

But I said, 'No. He didn't mean to do that to me. It was a mistake.' I felt so stupid. I felt it was all my fault. I shouldn't have bought the dress without asking him first. What had I been thinking?

*

I think I knew, deep down, that what he had done was wrong. I knew in my heart it meant he was violent, but I was stubborn, and I didn't want to believe it. I should have listened. I should have gone. But I didn't want to hear my parents saying, 'We told you so.' Besides, I really did not want to believe that my life was going to be like my mam's.

My head was saying, 'What are you doing? Your mother went through this, how can you go through the same?' But my heart was saying something different. Because when Barry wasn't hitting me, he was really lovely. He would be loving and sweet. It would be hugs and kisses. And it took me a while to just wake up and to realize that what Barry was doing to me was exactly the same as what my dad did to my mam.

I went back to work the following week. The girls were all asking me what had happened. I never took time out. They knew that. I just told them that I'd had a really bad cold. They accepted that. Or at least, they said that they did.

After a while, Barry started to meet me every day after work. The girls at work told me that it wasn't normal for a man to do that.

'We don't like him,' they'd say. 'Why is he always here? And why does he ask us so many questions?'

One Friday, Barry agreed to come out with us for a few drinks and he started to grill the other girls.

'Are there any men working in the factory?'

'No – well, there's Tony, our boss. And he's great!'

'In what way?'

'Well, he's not like you'd expect a boss to be. You can talk to him about anything.'

'Do you talk to any other men at work?'

'Only when we drop clothes off. Oh, that can be fun!' We

all giggled then. We loved it when we were sent over the bridge with a rail of clothes, to drop them in somewhere. It gave us a little bit of extra time to ourselves.

'Does Patricia often go up?' asked Barry.

'Oh, you go up for buttons sometimes, don't you, Trish?'

I nodded. I used to love that. There were a couple of lads who would chat to you. And of course the girls told Barry about that.

After that day, Barry began to come up to the factory at lunchtimes. He'd ask if I had to go on any errands. 'If you need to, I can walk you over,' he'd say.

The girls took me aside. They said they were worried about me. 'It's not right that he meets you like that, Trish. He's being too possessive,' they said.

I hated it when they criticized him like that, and the more they went on about how they didn't like him, the more I drifted away from the girls. I thought I knew better than they did. And I thought Barry was just being nice.

Then one Friday night my boss asked me and another girl to work late, and he asked a few of us to come in and work on Saturday. We'd get paid overtime, so of course we said yes. We had a big order to get out, and I was the only person who could do the buttonholes for the jackets.

I couldn't call Barry to warn him, so at five o'clock he was waiting for me as usual. I went down to explain to him I was working late. As I was talking to him my boss came down the stairs to get some sandwiches. Putting his hand on my shoulder, he asked me what kind of sandwiches I'd like. He was so kind. Such a lovely man. I told him what I wanted and introduced him to Barry.

'How do you do?' he said, shaking Barry's hand. 'I'm sorry you've had a wasted journey. I know I gave Patricia short

notice about the overtime, but I really need her on this job.'
He paused and smiled at me. 'Patricia is such a hard worker.'

Barry smiled, and said, 'Yes, Trish is great.' Then he turned
to me. 'Trish, I'll come back for you at about eight. Is that
OK?' I said it was. He did, and we went home. I was really
tired.

'I'm going to bed early,' I said. 'I've got a really early start
tomorrow, and I'm exhausted.' Barry seemed happy with
that. There wasn't a bother on him. So he changed, ready for
work, and kissing me, went out. I had a bath and got ready
for bed. Then the angels came to me. They said Barry had
locked the door with his keys.

I never had any reason to go to the door. It had a Chubb
lock, and I didn't really believe the angels. But I've always had
a fear of being locked in; I worry about not being able to get
out in a fire, so I took my keys to open the lock of the door.
But they didn't fit. My angel guide, Andrew, told me Barry
had changed the lock. I couldn't understand that. Why would
he do such a thing? It just didn't make sense. I was shaking
in fear.

I said to Andrew, 'This can't be right. Why would he
change the locks and not tell me?'

'Because he knows your fear.'

I was so worried. What if there was a fire? My angels came
into the room then. They calmed me down. They put their
healing wings around me, and I fell asleep.

The next morning Barry was asleep when I got up, but by
the time I was ready for work he was up.

'Barry, what happened to the lock?'

'What do you mean?'

'Have you changed it? My key wouldn't work.'

He stiffened, and looked uneasy. 'Why were you at the

door.' He looked angry, but didn't answer my question. 'Were you bringing people in as soon as my back was turned?'

I was puzzled. 'No. Of course not!'

'We'll talk about this later,' he said, and I agreed. I was already running late, and I hadn't time to argue just then.

So I said, 'Fine,' but said again that my key hadn't fitted the lock.

I ran for the bus, but I was feeling uneasy. And I felt even worse when Andrew and the angels warned me, yet again, that Barry was not good for me.

'Don't go back to the flat,' they said. 'Don't ever go back.'

My head was everywhere. In my heart I knew the angels were right. I remembered that Nan had said, 'Always listen to the angels.' She'd said they were always right and they were there to protect me. But why should I distrust Barry? Hadn't he always been good to me?

I couldn't concentrate at work. It was hard, because I knew how important it was to complete the order. As I was working on the final jacket, my mind wandered back to the lock. Why would Barry change it? What did that mean? Then I noticed I'd put the buttonhole in the wrong place. The minute I noticed I pushed the stop button on the machine, but it was too late. The jacket was ruined.

'I'm so sorry. So sorry,' I said to the boss. I was distraught. And he was furious. He was shouting at me, and he was normally such a patient man. I couldn't take it. I burst into tears. At that he looked horrified. He'd never seen me like that. It wasn't like me to make a mistake, and he'd never seen me so emotional. He didn't know what to do. Leaving me to it, he just walked off.

'That's it now,' I said to the girls. 'I'm going to get the sack.'

They came over to my machine and said, 'How did you do that?'

'I don't know. I feel so stupid!' I was still crying.

Then one of the girls gave me the shock of my life. She said, 'You know the way you talk to the angel things?' I looked at her with my mouth hanging open. When I didn't reply at once, she said it again. 'You know you talk to the angels?'

'How do you know that?'

'My friend Paula told me. She told me how you'd given her that message in the pub. You did, didn't you?'

'Well, yes. And they're not angel things. They're angels. But what do they have to do with me making a stupid mistake with that jacket?'

'Well, I was wondering . . .'

'Yes?'

'Couldn't the angels fix the mistake for you?'

I burst out laughing. 'No, they can't.' I spluttered it out through my tears. It was just the thought of the angels coming and fixing it. I laughed even more as we all looked at the ruined jacket.

Just then my boss came back. I was expecting him to shout at me again, but he seemed calm. He handed me a paper bag, and said, 'Take a break.'

'What? Now?'

'Yes. Sit down. Relax. And enjoy it, because when you come back you're going to have to work flat out. We *have* to get these orders out today.'

'OK.' I did as he said, but I wondered why he was now being so nice to me. And when I peeked into the paper bag and saw he'd bought me a custard slice, I was really pleased. I realized this meant he was sorry for making me cry. The custard slice was his way of making it up to me.

We'd rarely worked as hard as we did that day. But it was worth it. We got everything finished and that put us all into a really good mood. The boss was cracking jokes and we were all laughing. He was messing and saying, 'Who's the best boss?' and we were shouting back, 'You are!'

We were chatting, happily, as we went down the back stairs. As we rounded the final corner I saw Barry waiting for me. He didn't look happy.

'Sure, you have a great time in this job!' he said.

We all kept laughing. We felt so proud of ourselves for getting everything done. It had put us on top of the world.

'You *are* coming for that drink?' The girls were already heading off for the pub.

'Of course,' I said, starting to follow them, but Barry was shaking his head.

'No, Trish. We can't go. Have you forgotten I'm working tonight?'

'But Trish could still come,' shouted the girls.

I shrugged as Barry just dragged me away. We were quiet on the journey home. I was feeling angry. It was like he'd burst my bubble. I started thinking back to that morning. And when we arrived home, I brought up the locks again. That proved a mistake. Barry flipped.

'Why does that bother you so much?'

'You know why. I'm scared of being locked in. Suppose there was a fire . . .'

'Don't give me that.' Barry was shouting. 'It's because you have someone here when I'm out. Isn't it? Admit it now.'

'No!'

'Well, why did you check the lock?'

I didn't know how to answer. I hadn't told Barry that I

could see and hear angels. And if that wasn't bad enough, how could I tell him about Andrew, my spirit guide? I was silent for a while, trying to think up a good answer. I probably looked puzzled, but Barry decided it meant I was guilty of seeing another man.

He hit me. 'You're mine.' He shouted this out and landed another punch. 'Mine. All mine. Do you understand?'

He went on slapping me. Punching and hitting. I was getting the life kicked out of me. And I wasn't going to let him accuse me of something I'd never done.

'You ask me how I know about that stupid lock?'

'Well?' He aimed another kick at me.

'The angels told me.' I began to explain about the angels, and he stopped hitting me.

He looked at me in complete amazement, saying, 'What?'

I said it again. And again. Just to make sure that he understood. Meanwhile Andrew appeared and told me to stop talking.

'Don't tell him any more,' he begged me.

At that, Barry got hold of my hair and threw me down on the floor. 'Your dad warned me you were mad, you stupid bitch,' he said. 'And he's right!' He hunkered down and stared into my eyes.

'Where are your angels now? Why are they not helping you? If they're so clever, why are they not here protecting you?' Aiming a final punch, he walked off. I was in such pain. I just couldn't move. I lay there and just cried and cried. In the end I cried myself to sleep. And the next day he acted as if nothing had happened. I couldn't believe it.

I felt so ashamed then. But trapped too. I didn't know where to go for help, and I didn't want to admit, even to myself, that I'd made a mistake moving in with Barry. I had to miss work again. There was no way I could go in with a black eye and bloody nose.

In the end I had to leave my job altogether. I had to because Barry couldn't stand any other man to be around me. And that included my boss.

About three months after I'd moved into the flat with Barry, Mam came round. Barry was really friendly to her. He made her tea and asked her to stay for dinner.

'Thank you,' she said. 'That would be lovely, Barry.' He was being so charming to her and so nice to me. He was acting the perfect host. I just sat there and wished that Barry would go out. If he'd only go out for a minute, that would be all it would take for me to tell Mam what was happening to me. I knew if I told her, she would help me to get away from him. After all, she had been through the same thing often enough with Dad. But Barry seemed to sense this. He was careful never to leave us on our own.

The beatings went on. The angels wanted to help, but there was only so much healing they could give me.

'Leave him,' said Andrew. He said it time and time again, and the other angels said the same. And finally I told them I would. After all, I thought, I was having no life of my own.

I decided to leave on the Saturday evening when Barry was out at work. But first I had to get hold of the key because he locked me in every time he went out. I'd asked for my own set of keys, but he'd just laughed at me and said there was no way he'd help me to meet other men — these imaginary men in his head. I waited until he was getting ready for work. He was in the bathroom, and I found the keys in his jacket pocket. My heart was pounding and my hands were shaking. I had the keys but didn't know what to do.

'Leave now,' said the angels. 'Leave now while you can.'

I should have just run out of that door. But I didn't have anything packed. So I didn't. I waited. And when Barry came out of the bathroom he caught me with those keys dangling from my hand. He went crazy.

'What are you doing with those keys?' he said. I just stood there shaking and the blows rained down on me. It was the worst beating I've ever had. I blacked out at one stage, and I don't remember much about it. He kicked me in the head and face. He'd never done that before. He was in a rage that night. I don't think he even knew what he was doing. And he definitely didn't care.

I thought he was going to kill me. And the worst thing was that this time he just walked out and left me there, not knowing if I was dead or alive. He went out to work and left me unconscious on the floor. I had bald patches where my hair had been ripped out. I couldn't open my eyes. I couldn't move. I was just gone. There was blood coming from my ear.

I might have been there all night. Maybe I would have died. But I was lucky that night. My uncle Terry had decided to come and see me. He's more like a brother to me really, we're so close in age. I'd always got on well with him, and he'd been up a few times to see me since I'd moved in with Barry. Maybe he was checking up on me. If he was, he'd never have known there was anything wrong. Barry had always been charming to him, and had made sure there were cans of beer in the flat when he visited. He knew Terry didn't drink tea.

Terry told me later that he'd got this really strange feeling; a feeling that he was needed. When he arrived at the flat, he was knocking and banging on the door for ages. He was about to walk away, but something stopped him. He got this really strong urge to come in, and he kicked the door in.

He was so shocked when he found me. He called an ambulance, and I woke up in hospital. I know it was the angels who put that thought into his head, and I am really grateful to them. If they hadn't, and if he hadn't turned up that night, I don't believe I would be alive today.

9 Breaking Away

Oh Angel of God, my guardian dear, to whom God's
love commits me, here ever this day be at my side to
light me, to guard, to rule and guide. Amen.

When I woke, my eyes were so swollen I could hardly see.
My nose was swollen too, and I had great clumps of hair
missing. They were doing scans in hospital, and testing my
memory. They were worried about my head, and that attack
did have an effect on me. Even to this day I miss a word or
get tied up sometimes. I'd broken some ribs too. I had to
wear this corset, and I remember it was really sore, especially
when I laughed.

I was in hospital for nearly two weeks. Mam came to visit.
She was worried about me, and she asked me to go home
with her.

'What about Dad? Isn't he still angry with me?'

'No,' said Mam. 'He asked me to tell you to come home.
Don't worry about him!'

As for Barry, he never even appeared. Not once. And I
knew then that I was never going back to him. Not ever.

While I was in hospital I saw a social worker. She was helping me to get through the trauma. She explained to me all
about domestic abuse, and how abusers can manipulate their
victims. It all made sense, but I'd already made up my mind
to leave Barry anyway.

Dad didn't say a lot. He let me go home, but he took it all in his stride. I thought he'd take against Barry. I thought he'd say, 'I'm going to kill him,' but he never did. I was hurt by that. It was like he didn't take it seriously.

Other people did, though. The day before I was to leave hospital, the doctor came and spoke to me. He said that I should press charges against Barry. He'd reported the incident to the gardaí, and said they'd be coming to see me.

'It's terrible what he did to you,' he said. 'You're one lucky lady that you pulled through. You mightn't be so lucky next time.'

I felt he was right. So I agreed to report him. The gardaí were really good. They took down all the details, then they spoke to the doctor who'd looked after me.

I went home and began to recover. But a week later, who should arrive at Mam's house but Barry? I got a terrible shock when I opened the door and saw him there. I tried to slam the door, but he jammed his foot in the way, so I couldn't. I was shaking from head to foot, but there wasn't a bother on him.

'I want to talk to you, Trish,' he said. 'I want to talk to you in private.' He took hold of my arms, and pulled me. 'Come for a drive,' he said, trying to get me out to his car.

'I'm not going anywhere with you!' I shouted it, and tried to twist myself away from him, but he kept pulling at my arms. He was stronger than me, and by now he'd pulled me halfway down the drive. So I screamed then. And I went on screaming. I screamed so much that finally he let go.

I ran up the drive, desperate to get away from him, but he came after me, running even faster than me.

'I'm sorry, Trish,' he said, when he caught up with me. 'I'm sorry I hit you and it won't happen again. I didn't mean to do it.'

I just looked at him.

'I really miss you. Come home to me. Please. Everything will be different.'

Barry was like my dad. He could be really charming when he wanted something. I was almost taken in.

'How? How will things be different?'

'I'll never lock you in. Never. And I'll never hit you. That was a mistake. It won't happen again.'

He was so convincing. So persuasive. It would have been easy to give in to him. But my angels were there for me. They stood beside me and gave me all the strength I needed.

'No, Barry,' I said. 'I'm never going back to you. You almost killed me!' He took a couple of steps back in surprise. 'I mean it. I'm never ever going back to you. And if you *ever* try to come near me again I'm going to tell the gardaí. Do you understand me?'

He nodded and left. I hoped that would be the end of it, but it wasn't. Every day he would go up to Mam's house and try to see me. He kept on and on. And one day he asked me to drop the charges against him.

'No. I won't do that,' I said.

'Well, if you won't do that, I have no choice.' He grabbed my arms and held them so tightly that afterwards I noticed he'd bruised me. 'I'll burn down this house, and you'll die. And so will your mam, and all your brothers and sisters.'

I believed him. I really think he was capable of doing that, so what could I do? I knew this guy was completely mad. I would still have had to stand up in court, and say yes, he did threaten to burn down the house. My word against his, and he knew a lot of people. Even if he'd been in prison he would have carried out that threat. A lot of people were afraid of him and they would have carried out that threat for him, no problem.

I didn't want to drop the charges. It was the last thing I wanted. But I went to the gardaí station that evening.

'I'm dropping the charges against my boyfriend,' I told them.

The gardaí on duty put down his pencil, and sighed. 'I really don't advise you to do that,' he said. 'It's not wise. Not after the bashing he gave you.'

'But I want to drop them. I really do.'

'Now why would you want to do that?' he was looking straight into my eyes. 'Did Barry threaten you? Is that it? Is that what this is about?'

'No!' I couldn't admit that. How could I, when I knew Barry would get me one way or another? They kept on trying to persuade me. They really did not want to let me go. But after an hour they could see I wasn't going to change my mind.

'Then there's nothing we can do for you.' The gardaí shut the charge book with a bang.

I felt terrible walking out of the station that night. I knew it was wrong to drop the charges, but what else could I do? I believed Barry's threats. I knew he was capable of carrying them out. Or if he couldn't, he'd get someone else to do it for him. He had a lot of contacts in the criminal world.

I didn't see Barry for about a week after that. I was trying to get my life back together, and I'd found myself a new job. I was at home on the Saturday night. Dad had gone to the pub, and Mam, me and my brothers and sisters were in the sitting room. We were playing I Spy. The kids loved that. They always managed to make the game last for hours, yet there wasn't much at all in that room. It's just that nobody wanted to move anywhere else. It was warm in the sitting room with the fire lit, and the rest of the house was always freezing.

I heard a knock on the door. Nobody was moving off their chairs to open it. The moment anyone got up from a chair, one of the smaller kids would jump onto it from the floor. They were always watching, waiting for someone to move, and there'd be a free-for-all. I found that funny. They always did that, and you'd have trouble getting them out of the chair when you got back. That's why nobody answered the door.

In the end I got up, and said, 'OK, it looks like it'll have to be me answering that door. As usual!'

I could see the kids getting ready to leap up, so I added, 'And when I come back I don't want to see anyone on my chair.'

Their little faces fell. I was trying to hold my laugh in.

'Why should you get your chair back, Yaya? We never do.'

I smiled. 'Because I am the one who has jellies in my bag.' At that they all beamed at me. I really loved them. I thought, *Bless them, they are really good kids.*

I opened the door, but there was nobody there, so I went back into the sitting room. I began to share out the jellies. Then I heard another knock, knock. I was convinced it was John or Mark just messing, so I ran out, swung back the door, and said, 'Gotcha!' But there was no one there.

I was looking straight out, when I felt this strange, cold feeling on my temple. My whole body just froze. My angels and Andrew, my spirit guide, stood there looking at me. I said to them, 'What is going on here? Why do I feel so spooked?'

I hadn't seen Barry. Not until he stepped out from the side where there's a corner. It's like a blind spot. 'Don't move,' said the angels. 'Don't do anything.' I couldn't move, even if I'd wanted to. I didn't understand what was happening, but a cold chill ran down my spine. I still felt that chill on my temple. Then, finally, Barry spoke.

'Let's see if your angels can save you now.' It was then that I realized he was holding a gun to my head. The cold on my temple was the metal of the gun.

'You're going to come home with me,' he said. 'Dead or alive, it's the same to me.'

I closed my eyes, and heard the click of the trigger. Then nothing. I thought, *Am I dead or alive?*

'Well, what's it to be? Me or God?'

I closed my eyes again and said, 'I'm not coming with you.'

'Well, if I can't have you, I'm going to make sure that nobody else can have you either.' His voice chilled me. My whole body was trembling. I couldn't control the shaking. But I became really brave.

I said, 'If you're going to do it, just do it.'

He pushed the gun closer into my head. My whole life flashed before me. I'd heard that happened but never believed it. Now I did. Meanwhile Barry was laughing. Laughing out loud.

I said a prayer. 'Oh Angel of God, my guardian dear, to whom God's love commits me, here ever this day be at my side to light me, to guard, to rule and guide. Amen.'

I felt the coldness leave me. I opened my eyes and saw Barry walk away. I still couldn't move. I just stood there thinking, *Did that really happen?* I was in shock.

I went in, and the kids were still playing I Spy. They were oblivious to what had been going on outside and I couldn't say anything in front of them. I didn't want to frighten them. Not when they'd already had so much to deal with in their short lives.

Mam realized that something was wrong. She could tell from the look of me.

'Mam, would you like a cup of tea?' She nodded, and followed me into the kitchen.

'Patricia, what's wrong?' she asked. I just burst into tears. I poured out the story, but I was shaking so much I don't think she understood a word I was saying. It took me ages to calm down. Then I told her what had happened.

She was in shock. 'Shall I go to the callbox and ring the guards?'

I thought about it. But I couldn't face going through all that again.

'No, Mam. I can't. If I do that, he'll only harm you or the kids. I can't risk that.'

I couldn't sleep that night. I was too aware of every little sound. I just didn't feel safe and I kept looking out of the window. In fact I didn't sleep well on any night after that incident. I carried on working, and communicating with the angels. But I was so tired. Every day was a struggle for me.

Barry died in February 2010.

10 Lost and Found

I was still hearing the angels. They protected me. But
I was telling them to go away.

I never felt that Dad understood me. I think he thought of
me, always, as an extra pair of hands. He'd always relied on
me to help Mam, and when I wanted a bit of independence,
he didn't like it one bit. And he didn't like it at all when I
started going out. Having lived away from home, I was starting to stand up to him a little. Maybe I was trying to rebel.
One day I came home from work and found my clothes
strewn all over the front garden. That wasn't the first time.
Dad had a habit of doing that. And I knew, I just knew, that
he must be in one of his moods.

It was strange. I could leave for work in the morning, and
everything would be fine, but then something could happen
while I was gone. Dad would have been drinking, or maybe
he'd put a couple of bets on and lost. If that happened he
would come home and realize there were lots of little children in the house, but no money left. When he was in a
mood, he would take it out on me.

I didn't knock on the door. I'd learned by then not to do
that. If I did try and get in, he'd only slam the door. He'd
shout, 'Fuck off!' and Mam would side with him.

She'd say, 'Don't answer him back.'

And I learned not to, because if I did, he would take his temper out on her and the kids.

Anyway, that time, I picked up all my clothes from the garden – it didn't take long because there weren't many of them – then I put them all in a plastic bag and headed to the bus terminus. I took the bus back into town and went into a pub called the Plough.

It was a pub I knew well, though normally I'd go in just at the weekends. There'd be loads of young people in then, and I'd get chatting to them. The bar staff knew me well. When they saw me that night, with my plastic bag, they said, 'Ah, Patricia! You're not out on the street again?'

This time, however, I had nowhere to go. Nan was dead; I couldn't go to Barry – I'd do anything but that – and I didn't feel I could go to Nanny Chris either. I didn't want to involve her in any of this trouble. She would look after me, but if I went there she would have a go at my dad. And then he would take it out on my mam and the children would suffer. I wouldn't stay with any of the girls from work either. I didn't tell them I was homeless. My pride wouldn't let me.

It was so much worse this time, and I started to go on a downward spiral. From the day I left that hospital I had started to drink a lot. And it got much worse after all the trouble I had with Barry. I knew it was wrong, and I hated it when Dad did it. So I can't explain why I did it. I just did.

Maybe it was a way to make life seem a bit better. Dad was an alcoholic, and nothing seemed to bother him. I'd seen friends drinking and I thought, *I'll do it*. But the really stupid thing was that when I was drinking I didn't even like it. I didn't like the taste, but it numbed a lot of things. At the time I was laughing and joking. But inside I wasn't. Inside I was screaming. It wasn't what I wanted.

Life was horrible back then. I had nowhere to go and I slept on park benches. I slept anywhere I could find. One time I slept in a forest – well, it was really a field with lots of trees on the way out to Ballyfermot. It was the only place I could find. I slept in between the trees with my coat on the ground, but I had nothing covering me. It was cold and it was scary. I heard all sorts of little noises during the night. I'd hear a crackle and imagine it was rats running around, though I'm not sure it was. So then I would sit up and just be aware of the pitch darkness that was around me.

I was still hearing the angels back then. They protected me. At the same time, I was telling them to go away. I was very confused. But I knew, in my head, that everything was going to be OK. I'd keep telling myself that. In the morning I'd go into an early house. Some of the pubs back then would open at seven. I remember there was one near Moore Street. I think it's gone now.

I'd go into the toilet, so that I could have a wash, and I'd take my clothes into work. It never looked as if I'd been out all night. Nobody knew. I just accepted what was happening to me. I knew, for some reason, that I was going to have a hard life. But I also knew that in the end everything was going to be OK. There were nights I was so cold; it could be so hard. That time I was on the streets for maybe three weeks.

I'd go to the Plough every evening, and when I was hungry I'd go to the chipper. Or if I hadn't any money, I'd go round the corner from the pub, where there'd be this guy sitting on the pavement, peeling potatoes for a café. He'd sit there with this big bucket and I'd watch him. He knew me, and every now and then he'd go into the café and come out with a sandwich for me. I'd give him a cigarette in return. It was like, in a sense, he knew.

If I could have kept my wages, maybe I could have got myself a bedsit, but I was still supporting my mother, even though I wasn't living at home. Mam would meet me on a Friday after work. She'd bring my brothers and sisters with her. I loved seeing them – I missed seeing them. I missed them so much.

I don't know if she realized I was sleeping rough. I think she was afraid to see that I was. She didn't ask, because she was afraid of what she would hear. That is what I believe.

One evening I was in the pub. I was chatting away to some girls I didn't really know. It wasn't the usual crowd, so I was just sitting there with them. I noticed a girl about my age. She was joining in, but I could sense all this sadness all around her. I remember thinking, *Why am I seeing that?* I really did not want to start seeing things again. I was still so afraid that if I did, I'd be locked up in the hospital again. Anyway, the girl got up and went down to the toilet. As she left the room the angels appeared and told me to go to the girl. They said she was going to need some help.

I said, 'I'm not really hearing you. I'm not going back into that hospital for talking to you.'

'Patricia, we will never leave you. Although you may not talk to us for a while, we will always be here. And, Patricia, that girl needs your help. Please go to her.'

I could feel the tears in the back of my eyes, because I knew in my soul that the angels were right. But how could I risk it? If someone heard I'd been talking to angels again, I'd be going back to that hospital. I was so afraid someone would know. But at the same time, I couldn't let any harm come to this girl. So I got up and went down to the toilet. As I walked in, two girls were gossiping at the washbasins. They were saying what they'd do to this young girl. I was shocked to think that someone could even think of hurting someone just because they didn't like them.

I looked at them and said, 'All right, girls?'

They just looked at me and gave me a smile that I knew was false. They said, 'If you don't want to get hurt you'd better go away.'

Meanwhile the girl wouldn't come out of the toilet. I knew there wasn't really much that I could do, but I thought if I spoke up for her, it might make a difference. I was used to being hurt and I didn't like it. I knew how it felt to be really afraid.

I asked the girls why they wanted to hurt her.

'We don't like her.'

'But that's not right. How would you like it if someone did that to you?' They just laughed.

They said nobody was even brave enough to try it. I asked the angels, *What happens next?* Then I saw this absolutely beautiful spirit woman behind one of the girls. She was adorable. She was a gentle, gentle soul. I could see that she'd had a lot of trouble in her life and a lot of illness.

She told me she was very sad that her daughter was turning into a bully. She wanted it to stop. She felt she couldn't pass over properly because of the way her daughter was behaving. She asked me could I pass this message on. I was terrified to do this, but she asked me again. In my head was, *I am going to get locked up again.* But my heart knew it was the right thing to do. I said to myself, *One last time, then no more taking messages or talking to the spirit world.*

I told the girl her mother was with her. And that she wasn't happy with the way she was behaving and the person she was becoming. I was expecting a huge slap, to be honest. I told myself, *That's it.* If I get a slap it will have been worth it to have passed on this message for the woman in the spirit world. Plus it would mean they'd leave the girl alone.

I didn't get a slap. The poor girl was in total shock. She said she was very sorry, and she used always to feel her mam around her but had not felt her for some time. And now she knew why. And I thanked God that that girl was open to the spirit world. They apologized, and the girl came out of the toilet. She thanked me and asked me how long I'd been able to talk to dead people. I found that very funny and I started to laugh. She asked me why.

'It was the way you said dead people.'

She looked puzzled. 'Well, they are, aren't they?'

I suppose I'd never really thought of them as dead. So I told her, 'To me they are not dead. Because I see them as living spirits. And that's what they are.'

And she said, 'OK. Whatever. Whatever rocks your boat.' And I remember looking at her and thinking, *What a strange thing to say.* But I left it, and we went back to the bar.

'What's your name?' I asked her.

'Barbara, but Babs for short,' she said. Then she told me that she'd not been having a very good life recently. It turned out she'd been thrown out of home too. I realized then that was the sadness I had sensed around her. And she was thinking of going to stay in her aunt's flat in Ballymun.

'Why don't you come with me?' she asked.

'I don't know about that.'

'Well, why not? Surely you don't want to sleep on the street?'

'No. But I can't impose. How can I?'

'My aunt's great. She won't mind. And besides, I owe you.'

'You mean rescuing you from those bullies?'

'Yeah. And if you come with me you'd really be doing *me* a favour.'

'How do you make that out?'

'I've been putting off going to my aunt. It'll help me to have you with me. It'll kind of break the ice.'

It was strange. Barbara was not normally in the Plough. She just happened to go along that particular night. I firmly believe that our paths were meant to cross. Barbara was a lovely-looking girl. She was small with short auburn hair and big almond-shaped eyes. She was beautiful and compassionate too.

I was really worried about going to some stranger's flat, but Babs insisted. So off we went to Ballymun, and I was introduced to her aunt. Babs told her my story and how I ended up on the streets. Her aunt was lovely. She gave us a nice cup of tea and made us something to eat. Her husband and children made me feel so welcome. They told me to stay with them until I got sorted. I paid them some rent, but not much. They knew I couldn't afford a lot, because of having to give half my wages to Mam.

They gave me a good old lecture on drinking too. At that stage I'd go in the pub whenever I could. I'd drink pints of Harp when I had the money, and I'd always ask for a straw, because it made the drink last longer. They told me it wasn't good to be drinking as much as I was. And I listened to them. Because they weren't just having a go at me. They seemed to really care.

There was a really happy atmosphere in that house. Barbara and I walked in, and the first thing I noticed was how clean it was. It was lovely and homely too. And I just couldn't believe how warm it felt; not just physically, but emotionally too. It was amazing being with a family that actually cared for each other.

But best of all, they showed me to a bed with fresh sheets. It was like I was in a hotel. I was in heaven. At home I'd shared a bed with my sister. She had her first child when she was sixteen, and from that time until Liz left home, he was also in the room. So, nine times out of ten, my bed was the sofa downstairs. And it felt so good just to have a nice warm bed that night. I slept like a baby.

The next day myself and Babs headed for work. It was early June and Babs mentioned that her birthday was coming up on the thirteenth.

'That's funny,' I said. 'Mine is soon too. It's on the ninth.' I was going to be nineteen.

'But that's great.' She grabbed my arm and started jumping up and down. 'We can have a party!' I wasn't so sure that I wanted one, but there was no stopping Babs. So in the end it seemed easier just to agree. We settled on a pub in Ballymun. Babs came from the area. Her mam and dad lived in one of the private houses there, and her family were well known. So she knew a lot of people in Ballymun, but I only knew Babs and her aunt and uncle.

The week before our birthday Babs was so excited. She was going on and on about the party. I listened, and went along with the arrangements, but I wasn't bothered. I wasn't really like Babs. She just liked to party. Her aunt said I should ask along a lot of friends too, but again I didn't really know anyone, so I decided to leave it all up to Barbara. And because it would be all her friends, we decided the party should be on her birthday, on 13 June.

The day before the party, Babs was inviting anyone she could see. We'd be walking through the Ballymun shopping centre, and she'd shout out to people she knew. And then she'd introduce me, acting as if she'd known me for years.

And the funny thing was, it felt like she had. We got on just so well. It was like we were sisters. She was hilarious.

As we were passing Crazy Prices, we saw this middle-aged lady walking through. She was tiny. Babs shouted out, 'Hello, Lil,' and everyone looked round. The lady looked up, and called back, 'God, Babs, I haven't seen you in such a long time.'

Babs introduced me as an old friend of hers, and then she was asking, 'How's Stephen?' She was asking loads of questions about Stephen, and she seemed really animated.

'Stephen is in fine form,' said Lil. 'He's doing really well for himself.'

'That's great. Where does he work?'

'In Documation. You know, the computer company.'

'Please make sure Stephen knows about the party,' said Babs. 'Please make sure he comes. I haven't seen him in ages.' And all the while I was watching Babs's body language, and was thinking to myself, *Babs obviously likes this Stephen fellow.*

The night of the party arrived, and we were getting ourselves ready. It was such fun changing together. It was really lovely. Babs was so excited, and it was a real novelty for me. I wasn't used to doing what I wanted to do. Babs had given me lots of advice on what to wear. I wasn't used to wearing dresses. I'd been put off wearing them because of the way Barry had carried on over the last dress I had got. Yet I loved making myself look nice.

I wore a figure-hugging cream dress that night. I wasn't sure about it at first, because since Barry I'd been a devil for wearing black. I hardly ever wore other colours, but Babs told me it looked really good.

In the end I loved that dress. My hair was really long back then. It came down below my waist. I really felt like a queen that night. But just before we left for the pub, Babs asked me if I was OK. She had noticed that my hand was shaking. And I *was* nervous. I wasn't used to being around a lot of people. I'm a very private person.

'No. I'll be fine,' I said, and she gave me a quick hug. She knew what was behind my nerves. I'd told her all about Barry.

Anyway, myself and Babs went over to the Penthouse. There was a roar as we arrived. Babs seemed to know everybody in the pub. People were coming up to her saying how nice it was to see her and how great she looked. And she did. Her red hair was shining, and her eyes looked huge with the make-up she'd put on. Some of her friends hadn't seen her for a long time. She was so happy to see them all again. She was all bubbly – she loved being the centre of attention. She was very outgoing and jokey, especially now that her life was going so much better, and she was good for me too. I wasn't so shy when I was around her.

Babs introduced me to everyone and told them it was my birthday too. That made me a bit embarrassed. Even though she was chatting away, Babs kept looking at the door. Every single time it opened, she'd turn and look. She'd be chatting and joking and laughing but, sure as God, as soon as the door opened her eye caught it. I wondered why, and I asked her.

'Oh! I'm waiting to see if Stephen turns up.'

'I knew it!' I said. 'I knew you liked him.' I started teasing her then, and slagging.

'No. We're just friends,' she said, but she blushed.

'Go on out of that! I've never seen you like this before.'

'No, really! I've known him forever. We grew up together and we were really close. But we were never more than friends. It's just that I haven't seen him for a while.'

Eventually Stephen arrived. I knew it must be him, because the minute he walked in Barbara ran over and gave him a big hug. I remember looking at them and thinking, *God, they look so sweet together.* She brought him over to our table and introduced us. He was nice. He was really chatty. He could talk for Ireland, and everyone in the pub seemed to know him. I remember looking at him and thinking that he must've kissed the blarney stone when he was still in the womb, because this had to be the only person I knew who could talk so much.

'Isn't Stephen great?' Babs said to me. And I agreed he was, because there was something really attractive about him. I thought, again, how good he and Babs looked together. Then she started stirring. She said, 'Trish, he really likes you.'

'Oh, Babs, stop that!' I couldn't understand why she'd even say it, when it was so obvious that she liked him. 'I'm not ready for anything like that. Not right now. The last thing I need is a man in my life. And anyway,' I said, pretending not to care either way, 'how do you know he likes me?'

'He told me.'

'You mean he does take a breath.' I was laughing now.

She started laughing. 'Will you just stop! But he and you would get on just great. I know you would. I can feel it in my water.' I started laughing again. She looked at me then.

'Why don't you ask the angels?'

'Oh, Barbara. I don't talk to the angels any more. I told you.'

At the end of the night Babs asked her aunt was it OK to bring some friends back to the flat and she said, yeah, of course it was. I think her aunt was a party animal too. So off we went with a couple of drinks in our hands.

Stephen came back. So did a few of his friends. He knew Babs's family very, very well. I think he'd worked with her dad at one stage. It was lovely sitting there in the flat. There was no messing. Nobody was slagging anyone else or fighting. Everyone was in good form. And there were no arguments. I wasn't used to that. We were just sitting, talking in general, and listening to music.

And then we all had a sing-song. I was sitting on the side of an armchair, and I was tapping out the rhythm, as if I was banging a drum.

Stephen turned to me and said, 'Do you like drumming?'

'Oh, I'd love to play the drums,' I said. And we started talking about music. Stephen seemed to know so much about it. But then he seemed to know so much about everything. I really liked that about him. It was a really good night.

We were all sitting there having a good old chat when one by one people started to leave. It was the early hours of the morning by then. Before I knew it everyone had gone and it was just Stephen and me talking. I had to laugh. I'd been going on about what a talker he was, and there I was waffling the ears off him. We were still there at five in the morning.

When I looked at my watch I couldn't believe it. I was in shock. I had never ever talked to someone for so long. At least not anyone except for the angels and the spirit world. But I didn't think anything about it. Stephen was nice. I really liked him, but he was friendly with everybody. He was just so down to earth.

11 Stephen

Angels are our constant companions.

The next day Babs asked me if I was going to see Stephen again.

'No, I am not!' I was emphatic. 'There is *never* going to be a man in my life. Not after Barry.'

'Oh, right. So you're going to be a nun, are you?'

I laughed. 'Now that's not such a bad idea.' I took a drag from my cigarette. 'But first, I'm going to go to Crumlin to see my uncle.'

'What, the one who lives with your Nanny Chris?'

'That's the one.' I was really fond of Uncle Sean. He was more like a brother to me than an uncle. He's only five years older than me, and he still lived with his mam and dad.

'Don't go, Trish. Not today. Stay, and let's have some fun.' Babs begged and begged me, but I felt I *had* to go. I hadn't seen Sean or my grandparents for a couple of weeks.

'Nanny Chris will have words with me if I leave it any longer. Let me tell you, Babs, Nanny Chris is *not* a woman you'd want to get on the wrong side of.'

'But why today? Won't it wait until next week?'

'Not really,' I said. 'I haven't told her yet that I've been put out of the house.'

'Why not?'

'Oh, you know. Families.'

'What's she like, Nanny Chris?'

'She's really young and modern. She's really into fashion. You'd like Nanny Chris. She's feisty. But if she hears from someone else that Dad threw me out of the house, and that I'm now living with strangers in Ballymun she'd have a fit. And she'd go and have words with Dad.'

'Would that be so bad?' Babs just didn't get it.

'Yes, that would be bad. Because then he'd just take it out on Mam. Really, Babs, this is important. She needs to know that I'm OK, and have somewhere really nice to stay. Then she'll be happy.'

Babs, though, just wasn't going to take no as an answer.

'Trish, one more week won't hurt. And next week I can come along with you. Then your Nanny will know that you're in good hands here. Please? Stay here with me. Then we can talk about the party.'

In the end she wore me down. Babs was good at that. And I thought it would be nice, just to stay in, relax, and go over everything that had happened at the party. But it turned out that Babs had different ideas. She wanted to go out that night, and I really didn't want to. I was tired. It had been such a late night. I was still on my tablets too, and they didn't help. Neither did the drink. All I really wanted to do was to go to bed and sleep.

But Babs begged me and begged me. She said it would be no fun going out without me, and finally she convinced me.

'OK,' I said. 'I'll come, but I'm not staying out late. And I'm not having a drink either.' Babs raised her eyebrows. 'I don't feel like it, and if I don't get an early night I'll be wrecked for work in the morning.' Babs was doing a little dance of celebration.

'Where are we going, anyway?'

'Oh. The Penthouse.'

'The Penthouse?' I gave her a look. 'Again? Why are we going there?'

'Because I like it.'

I knew, then, that she was up to something. She had to be. She was getting all giddy like a bold child. And I couldn't help but laugh at her. We got on great.

'It's handy,' she said. 'It's just across the road.'

'Come on, Babs, what are you up to? I know it's something. You just can't hide that cheeky smile of yours.'

Anyway we went over and Babs got a glass of Harp and I got a glass of 7 Up.

Babs said, 'Ah, Trish, come on. You're not only having that.'

'I am. I had to take the Valium, and I'm not going to drink.' I started to get an uneasy feeling. It was like I could sense someone or something. But for the life of me I couldn't figure out what it was. Barbara was very understanding. She knew I'd had a really bad time. She knew all about my family, and she was great at saying the right thing at the right time.

When I'd finished my drink, I told Babs I was going home now. She looked frantic, and told me to have just one more 7 Up. I agreed. And as she came back from the bar, who should walk in, but Stephen. He walked straight over to our table. Babs was giddy and I knew she had planned all this. I sensed, too, that it wasn't because she liked Stephen.

It was funny. I was so scared of men. To me they just meant trouble. After Barry, I really didn't want a boyfriend, but Stephen was different. I could talk to him, and I didn't feel afraid. It was like I could tell him anything. So when he turned to me and asked me out, I found myself agreeing.

'I knew you two were right together,' said Babs later, as we headed home.

I just smiled. 'But why did you arrange tonight?' I asked.

'Stephen asked me to.'

'He did?'

'Yeah.' She hit me lightly on the arm, giggled and ran ahead. I ran after her, laughing. 'He rang this morning,' she said, out of breath now.

'But why the secrecy?'

'He thought if he asked you straight, you'd get scared and say no.'

I nodded, and admitted that perhaps I might have. It had been good, meeting him again with no pressure.

The next night Stephen and I met again. But this time we were by ourselves. It was strange. A week before – even two days before – that would have scared me. But it was like I was a different person. Stephen made me different. I could tell him everything. I explained all about Dad, and then I told him about Barry. And he just hugged me and said I was safe with him.

'Trish, you've just been unlucky,' he said. 'Most men *aren't* like that. Anyway, I'm not.' And I knew it was true. And from that day, we just hit it off. Three days later we went to the cinema. That was a big thing for me. I normally wouldn't go into picture houses. I hadn't liked to since the Dublin bombings. After that day, being in a dark space made me feel trapped. But with Stephen, I felt I would be OK.

Stephen took me to the Carlton Cinema in O'Connell Street. When I saw where we were I felt excited.

I left Stephen in the queue, and said, 'Wait here a minute,' and I ran into the cinema. Uncle Paddy worked there, and I went to see if he was around. And he was.

'Patricia!' He held out his arms, and gave me a hug. 'How are you?' He stood back and looked me over. 'Or need I ask? You look wonderful. Are you here to see a film?'

I nodded. 'I am. But I've got a chap with me.'

'Oh, you've got a man with you, have you?' He raised his eyebrows at that, and let out a sharp laugh. 'Well, I'd better come down the queue and check him out then, hadn't I? I'd better make sure he's OK.'

I don't know what Stephen must've thought when he saw me appear with Uncle Paddy. He's a big man, and looked like he could be a bouncer. When I introduced him Stephen looked relieved.

'You've a nice firm grip, young man,' said Uncle Paddy. 'That tells me you're a nice strong person.' Stephen gave me a look, and I started laughing. Uncle Paddy said, 'Come this way. I can't have Patricia standing out in the queue.' And he brought us up past everyone who was queuing and gave us the very best seats in the house. I felt so important. I thought, *This is great*. As for Stephen, he was delighted.

He said, 'That deserves a bag of chips now on the way home.'

I laughed. 'It does?'

'Yes. Because I didn't have to pay for you to get in.' We laughed and joked about that. It was so easy being with Stephen. We could talk about absolutely anything. We had this really strong connection.

Stephen was determined to get me to speak to Dad.

'You really must,' he said. 'It's not good to fall out with your family. Not good, whatever they've done.'

I didn't want to. I really didn't, but I could see he was right. And besides, I wanted to see Mam. I'd really missed all my brothers and sisters.

'OK,' I said. 'We'll go.' I didn't say it, but I was praying that Dad wouldn't be there. We went on the bus. Stephen was holding my hand tightly. He knew I was nervous. I didn't say a word. Not that you'd have noticed, as Stephen kept up the chat, just as he always did. We got off the bus and walked down the pavement towards our house. As we got close, I had butterflies in my stomach. I was terrified.

When I saw the gate ahead of us, I stopped dead, turned to Stephen and said, 'I don't know if I can face this.'

'Face what?'

'I can't go in there.'

'Come on, Trish.' Stephen looked at me.

'Well, not without taking a Valium first.'

'It's that bad?' I nodded, and scrabbled in my bag for my pills. I downed one without water. Stephen looked sad. He didn't want me to take one. He didn't like me taking any of my pills, but he understood. He knew that I had so many bad memories of that house; he knew I'd left it in terrible circumstances, and thought that, at the sight of it, everything would come flooding back to me.

But to be honest, that's not the real reason I was so terrified. What really frightened me was that Stephen would turn and run the other way as soon as he walked in that door. I'd explained about my family, but it's different when you see the situation. There were so many problems in my family. And I really would not have blamed him if he had run.

After all, it would make him realize that he wasn't just taking on me. He was taking on a whole load of baggage. When we got to the door, though, I forgot all my worries. My heart just melted. Because there, peeking through one of the side windows of the door, was Bridget. She was such a tiny tot. And I could see her giggling and giggling. Her big brown eyes were shining. We could hear her shouting in excitement.

'Yaya's here, Yaya's here. Open the door, here's Yaya.'

Poor Stephen didn't know what had hit him. All the kids were crowded at the door. There was a massive scramble, as they fought over who would be the first to see me again. I must admit I was excited to see them all again. Their little faces were looking up at me, and they were so happy. I gave them all the sweets I'd bought for them, and that made them even happier.

Mam, though, looked really tired. She was expecting another baby, and my heart just sank. It really did. Dad wasn't at home and I thanked God for that. I loved Dad. Even after everything that had happened I still loved him. But he had a fierce temper on him, and that was the thing that really frightened me. If Stephen set eyes on him, I felt sure he'd turn and run. Without Dad there, I could start to relax a bit.

Mam and Stephen seemed to get on really well. It was easy really. Stephen was doing all the talking, chatting away to Mam. The kids took to him too. They loved him. They were clambering all over him, with their sticky fingers. He didn't know where to put himself.

I said, 'Have you ever seen so many children together in the one room?'

And he said, 'No. But I can see that you love them very, very much. And I can see that they love you too. They have obviously missed you.'

'Oh, they have,' said Mam. 'Well, we all have. And quite honestly, Trish, I could do with your help. Would you not come home again, at least until the baby has arrived?'

'When is it due?'

'In the next couple of weeks, and I don't mind telling you it worries me.'

'But, Mam, I'm really happy. I'm living in this wonderful flat, and I've made this friend, Barbara. She's lovely. She's helped me so much.'

Mam started crying. I looked at Stephen, and sighed. I never liked to see my mam upset.

I said, 'Well, let's see what Dad has to say.'

I left then, but not without promising to visit her again very soon. And Stephen and I went back to Ballymun. I was really worried and we had a good old chat on the bus.

Stephen said, 'Would you not go back home to your mam? I can see she really badly needs you there. She's really tired and needs your help.'

I had to think hard about it. I felt my life was just starting to get back together again. I felt happy and I felt free, and that was new to me. Yes, I was still on the medication. Yes, that bothered me, but apart from that, my life was starting to be my own. At the same time, I couldn't get the picture of my Mam out of my head. When we got back to the flat in Ballymun, I spoke to Babs about it.

'That's awful,' she said, but I could tell she wasn't really listening. She wasn't her usual bubbly self, and it turned out that she had her own problems.

'What's up with you, Babs?'

'Oh, I had a row with my aunt. A bad one.' After that things started to go downhill. The family were still good to me. They still made me feel welcome, but the atmosphere just wasn't the same. It felt strained.

I decided I had to go back to talk to Mam and Dad. Dad didn't exactly welcome me with open arms – that wouldn't be his way, but he did tell me that I could come back home.

I don't think it was that he missed me. What he missed, I think, was the few bob I brought in. And then there was all the work I did cleaning around the house, and taking care of the kids. He could be wise when he needed to be. And he knew he'd need someone there when Mam went in to have the baby. There was nobody else, as Liz, the next sister down, had left home when her baby was a toddler.

'Could my friend Barbara come and stay too?' I asked.

'And why should we have a stranger in our house?'

'Well, because I don't want to leave her out on the street. She rescued me once, remember?'

So Babs came to stay, and we both continued going in and out of work. It was great having her there to help. We were like wizards running around cleaning when we got in from work. The kids really loved Barbara. She was a great messer, more so than I was, and they loved the way she clowned around with them.

Then one day Dad got into one of his bad moods again. We got up the road and there were all our clothes in the garden.

I sighed, and said, 'Barbara, I can't keep doing this.'

I meant it. I really couldn't face being out on the streets again. So this time I swallowed my pride, and we went off to my Nanny Chris in Crumlin. I explained everything to her. She wasn't happy.

'Trish, this isn't good,' she said. 'Not when your mam is about to have the baby.' She took me into another room, shut the door, and said, 'That Barbara is a bad influence on you, Trish.'

'Nan, that's not true,' I said, and I laughed. She was so wide of the mark.

'You can stay, Trish. Of course you can.' I flung my arms around her, but she pushed me gently away. 'But not your friend.'

'But Nan . . .'

'No.' She put up her hand in a stop signal. 'You're not getting round me. I don't care what you say, I'm not having your friend in this house.'

I didn't know what to do. I couldn't leave Babs to fend for herself. That didn't seem fair when she'd been so good to me. Then I had a good idea. I remembered John, who lived across the road from Nan's. He was like a brother to me. He and Uncle Sean grew up together. John's mam and dad had died when he was in his teens, and Nanny Chris had helped to bring him up. I had always got on very well with him. I took Babs over to meet him, and they hit it off at once. Babs really liked him. So she ended up staying in his house, and I stayed with Nan.

Soon after we'd moved into the houses, we got the news that Mam had had her baby. It was a girl. They called her Lisa. She was born on 20 July 1980, about a month after I met Stephen. I went up to St James's Hospital to see my little baby sister in the maternity unit there. I was so excited – so looking forward to seeing the baby, but it turned out that Dad was still in one of his rages, and he refused point-blank to let me see her. I was devastated. All I wanted to do was see them.

After a few days, Mam came out of hospital, and I went out and bought the baby's pram. I wheeled it up to the house, and Dad let me leave it outside. But he wouldn't let me go in. He wouldn't even open the door.

'Dad, please!' I said. 'Please let me see my sister.' But he was having none of it.

Finally, after a couple of weeks, he calmed down and let me see her. I'll never forget my first sight of her. She was sitting on Mam's knee. She was so tiny, and she was absolutely gorgeous. She had a mop of black hair. Mam passed her to me, and I hugged her.

'Look at her tiny hands,' I said, and counted her little fingers. Poor Mam was so tired though. She had a one-year-old as well as this new baby and a two-year-old, and it was too much for her. She asked me, again, would I come home.

One day in September, I was sitting in Nanny Chris's kitchen. I'd just got back from work, and was having a cup of tea.

Stephen walked in, and said, 'How's about you and me getting married?'

I just burst out laughing, and said, 'The next point is?'

'No, Trish. I'm serious,' he said, and he did look it.

But I just laughed and laughed. 'You and your jokes,' I said. 'You're just brilliant at cracking jokes.'

He sat down beside me then, and took my hands. 'I'm glad someone thinks it's funny.' He looked fed up. 'How can I convince you I'm serious?'

I stopped laughing then, and looked at him. Could he really mean it?

'You really are serious?'

He nodded.

'Well then, yes!' I started to laugh again. But this time it was because I was happy. He really did want to marry me? Even when we'd known each other such a short time? It was quite a shock. I couldn't believe it. I think it was the way he asked me, because he can be kind of cheeky.

Fair play to Stephen, he decided to do the right thing. He asked me to arrange a meeting with my dad.

'OK, but you'd better be prepared for his temper,' I said.

'Why? Aren't I good enough for you?'

I laughed. 'Too good! Dad usually only gets on well with drinkers. They're his friends.' Anyway, he went to Mam and Dad's house without me one day, and he asked for my hand in marriage. To my surprise, my dad agreed. Myself and Stephen went into town together and chose the ring. It was gold with a single diamond. I loved it! We decided to marry the following March, and we started saving for the wedding.

It was agreed that Stephen's parents and mine would club together and pay for half of the wedding, and Stephen and I would pay for everything else. But we hadn't really got enough money, so we both took on extra jobs. Stephen ended up with three jobs, and I had two, and we saved every penny.

Life was mad for a few months. I moved back home with my parents. Stephen and I didn't get to see one another very often. We were, literally, passing each other, but when we *did* see each other, you know, we were happy. We were fine. We knew, always, that getting married was the right thing. I never had any doubts.

When we were going to get married, I went into town to get my birth certificate, and they couldn't find one. They said I didn't exist.

'What? I don't exist? I'm here, aren't I?'

I went back home then to Dad, and he said, 'I'll sort it.' I don't know how he did it. He had to go through all kinds of rigmarole, but he did sort it in time. I was puzzled though.

'Dad, why didn't you register me?'

He shrugged. 'I thought the nurse had done it. I thought that was what happened when a baby was born at home.'

I'm still not quite sure which year I was born. Mam and Dad have always insisted it was 1961, two months after they married, but Nanny Chris never agreed.

'Don't you remember, John?' she said to my dad. 'You

went to the Congo *after* Patricia was born. Don't you remember those lovely baby dresses you sent home?'

Myself and Stephen didn't see each other too often around that time. We were too busy working to save all our money for the wedding. But on Valentine's Day we decided we deserved a good night out. There was a big night planned at the Stardust Disco on the Kilmore Road. Stephen and myself liked going there, so we bought some tickets. Liz was going to come too, and her friend.

I was working for a security firm. I used to get paid by cheque and one of the local shops in Edenmore used to cash my wage cheque for me every week. On that Friday I went in as usual. The girl who cashed my cheque was a good friend of mine. We used to meet up at the Stardust for a drink every now and again. On that Friday she said to me, 'Are you going tonight?'

'Bloody right I am. I wouldn't miss it for the world.'

'Are you going with Stephen?'

'Of course I am!' I laughed. 'He's calling down for me.'

'That's right. Sure, it's only a month away from you getting hitched.' With that, she asked me could she borrow my ring. 'Please, please let me borrow your ring. I want to let on to all the lads that I am engaged and getting married. I'll give it back to you later when I see you!'

That took me by surprise. 'Oh, go on, then. But don't lose it. Stephen will go bleeding mad if I lose that ring.'

I came out of the shop and walked up the road. Then I thought, *Oh, the engagement ring. What'll I do if she does lose it?* I didn't want to risk it. So I turned round and went back into the shop.

'Look, I tell you what,' I said. 'I'd be terrified you'd lose the ring.'

'Oh!' she said. 'In the space of two minutes I've told about ten people I'm engaged.' She took another look at her finger with the ring on. Then, sighing, she pulled it off, and gave it back.

'Look, I'll see you there tonight. And I'll let you wear the ring for the night.' We both had a good laugh then.

I went home and got ready. Stephen called round to the house, and Liz and myself came downstairs, dressed up and ready to go. Liz had brought my young nephew over to the house earlier, as Mam was babysitting for her. We were all walking out the door to go to the Stardust.

'Enjoy it,' said Mam. Then she turned to Liz and said, 'And don't forget you're a mother.' It was just a casual comment, but Liz looked annoyed. She muttered, 'As if you'd let me forget.'

Dad walked into the sitting room at precisely that moment and he just flipped. He looked at Liz and said, 'Your mam's not babysitting for you. You're not going.'

We all looked at Dad in surprise. This was unusual. Liz was never stopped from going out whenever she wanted. She was sobbing.

There was a bit of an argument and Dad said, 'There's nothing stopping you and Stephen from going.'

'Well, I'm not going if Liz is not going.' I thought Dad was being unfair. I had a pain at the pit of my stomach. It was because of all that tension. Dad did, eventually, give in to Liz. But that was two hours later. At that stage she said she didn't want to go.

'But you go, Trish,' she said. 'I don't want to spoil it all for you and Stephen.'

So the two of us headed out, but the mood had gone off us.

'I'm not going at this time of night,' I said.

'You're right. It's too late now.'

'Let's just go into town.' So we did. But we didn't tell Mam and Dad we'd changed our plans. We went for a drink. After having a couple of drinks, myself and Stephen headed back to the house where Stephen was supposed to have been working that night. We let the guy who was standing in for him go instead. It was this corporation house that was being renovated. Back then, they put in security to stop squatters from moving in, and Stephen worked for the security firm.

It was strange. Normally we would turn the radio off at night, but for some reason we had left it on that night, and the next morning we woke to hear the tragic news that there'd been a fire in a disco. Lots of people had been burned to death and injured. And worst of all, many people had been trapped. They'd struggled to get out, but the exit doors had been chained. At first we thought this was in another country.

Then we heard the words 'Stardust' and 'Dublin'. Shivers went down my spine. As far as everyone was concerned, we had gone there.

Stephen went home to his mam, and I went to my mam's. Dad wasn't there. He was already up at the Stardust looking for us. Of course we weren't there. We were so lucky that night. So lucky.

Forty-eight people died in the Stardust fire. And that included the girl who wanted to borrow my ring. It was so sad. Myself and Stephen were the lucky ones. We came home. They never came home.

I was so excited about going there that night. I was really looking forward to it. I'd been there many a time before. I don't know why I decided to stand up for Liz. I'm now convinced it was the angels' way of keeping me away from the Stardust. It wasn't my time.

Everyone was walking around in a daze of disbelief after that night. I knew a family of three who died, as well as the girl in the shop. A few others I knew, just to see, died too. I've never been to so many funerals in such a small space of time.

You could feel the sadness around Edenmore and Coolock. Everyone was wondering, *Why?* How could something like that happen, and all because they chained the doors so that people wouldn't get in for nothing? It was horrible.

We've never celebrated Valentine's Day since that day. We just couldn't. I light a candle for the forty-eight. I never forget.

Everyone in the family was excited about the wedding. There were relatives in and out of the house. My sisters were really excited about being bridesmaids. One of them was going on and on about it. She was going on and on to Dad about a pair of shoes she wanted. This was a week before the wedding.

I had already bought all the bridesmaids' shoes, but my sister wanted ones with a higher heel. She kept on asking Dad.

'You've already got a pair,' he said. He was drinking that day. 'And anyway, we don't have the money.'

'Please, Dad. Please.' She just wouldn't leave the subject alone. I was in the kitchen at the time, and suddenly I heard this commotion. There was all this shouting.

'What's going on?' I asked, and Mam's younger brother – he was there that day – started shouting.

'He's burning the money.'

'What?'

'The wedding money. He's throwing it on the fire.' I rushed

into the sitting room, and sure enough, there was this bundle of notes on the fire. And it included the money I had given Dad for our half of the reception.

'Dad? What did you do that for?'

Sean was trying to pull the money out of the fire. 'Trish, it's the wedding money. It's the wedding money.' I grabbed the poker and joined Sean. We were tossing notes out of the fire. Dad ignored us. He didn't even speak. He just walked off. He slammed the door and went down to the pub. We didn't see him until after closing time.

We got most of the money out of the fire. There was £900 in the bundle, and we saved all but £200.

'What was that about?' I asked, once we'd counted the money. 'Surely not just about a pair of shoes?'

'Well, that was the start,' said Sean. 'Or rather the end – the last straw. Your dad was raging. He just lost it. He said, "I'm sick of it. You want this and you want that." He was on about your sister. He said, "There's going to be no fucking wedding," and that's when he threw the money in.'

I thought, *My God, what are we going to do?*

'Where are we going to get the money from?'

Sean just shrugged.

'I'll go and ring Stephen,' I said. But we didn't have a phone. And, of course, back then, we didn't have mobile phones. So I walked up the road to the callbox. I rang Stephen's work, and asked them could he contact me somehow on his break. He just got on his motorbike and came up. I was still distraught.

I was sobbing. I said, 'There's not going to be a wedding.' He just said, 'Don't worry. We'll sort it out.'

And we did. We both worked extra hours.

*

I'll never ever forget my wedding day. It was so very special. Nanny Chris came to the house in the morning, to help me get ready. My godmother was there too. She'd come over specially from England, and she'd brought her children with her. They were all there in the bedroom with me.

I remember my godmother was doing my hair. She'd finished, and she was about to put in my veil when there was a knock on the door.

Mam said, 'Who is it?'

'It's me.' It was Granddad.

Nanny Chris snorted. 'Tommy,' she said. 'You're not allowed in here. You're not allowed to see the bride.'

'Please,' he said. 'Please let me be the first.'

'What do you think, Trish?' My godmother was flicking the veil in place. 'Can he see you?'

I nodded. One of my cousins opened the door. Granddad came in. Tears filled his eyes.

'You just look beautiful.' He took my hand.

That set me off. 'Granddad. You're going to spoil my make-up.'

'You've made me the proudest man ever.' He squeezed my hand. 'I just want you to be happy.' He wiped a tear from his eye, turned around, and went down the stairs.

Everybody left for the church then. Dad and I went down the stairs and out of the house. And there, lined up in the garden, were all these little children who lived on the road. Each one of them held a daffodil.

I loved those kids. I knew them well, because I babysat most of them. I used to bring them up to the shops, and if I had spare money I'd always buy them something. Their mams had decided to make that guard of honour as a thank you to me. That really got me. There they were standing in my mam's garden. I just wanted to burst into tears. They were like little angels standing there.

We arrived at the church, where the bridesmaids were waiting for us. My sister Liz was the chief bridesmaid, and Stephen's sister was the other bridesmaid. Mark was a little pageboy, and Bridget and Margaret were my flower girls. The church was full. We had 120 guests, because we both have such big families. The day went really well. Dad had been drinking in the morning and he wasn't sober when he walked me down the aisle, but there weren't any nasty scenes. He gave a speech. He didn't say much. I think he was too drunk at that stage, but he got through it OK.

The wedding reception was in the Ormonde Hotel, down on the quays. Stephen and I were booked in there, too, to stay that night. But when I went up to change I checked the bed and noticed somebody had been playing practical jokes. They'd done an apple-pie bed. That made me suspicious, and I then heard some muffled giggling. I told Stephen.

'A couple of our mates are hiding in the wardrobe,' I told him.

'Is that so?' He laughed. 'Hey, Trish, we'll show them.'

We went back to the room together, pretending that we were about to go to bed. Then Stephen put a finger to his lips and shushed me. Taking care to keep really quiet, we took all our things and sneaked out of the room while they were all still hiding there. Then we walked round the corner and booked ourselves into a bed and breakfast. And that's where we spent the first night of our marriage.

12 Marriage and Babies

I never told Stephen about the angels. Not a whisper. I
was scared he would think I was mad and would leave.

The day after our wedding we got the bus from town to
Edenmore, because we couldn't afford a taxi, and when we
got in there, my mam and one of my aunties were still in bed.
The kids were running around everywhere, and there was no
sign of my dad. I went up the stairs and into Mam's room.
When my auntie opened her eyes, she looked at me and
closed her eyes again. Then she opened them again.

'You did get married yesterday?'

'Well, I should hope so!'

She was so hung over. When she and Mam got up, I
noticed Mam was limping.

'Are you OK?'

'I think it was the new shoes,' she said. 'I'm not used to
them. I think they've cut my feet.'

'Where's Dad?'

'I haven't got a clue.'

My auntie was holding her head and groaning. She said
she needed a cure. So we all went to the Concorde pub up
the road from my mam's. All the staff there were looking at
me funny, and I hadn't a clue why.

I kept saying to Stephen, 'Why are they looking at me like that?'

'It could be because they know you got married yesterday.'

'Could be.'

Then in walked Dad, and he looked at me and went, 'Yaya.'

'Oh, there you are!'

'Come here. Now.'

I went over and he said, 'You're not supposed to be here.'

'Why?'

'I told them all you were going to Spain for two weeks, so fuck off wherever you're going. And don't bother coming back here for two whole weeks.'

'But I'm going to come back with no tan.'

'I don't give a fuck,' he said. 'I'm not having anyone thinking my daughter didn't go on honeymoon because we couldn't afford it. So keep away from Edenmore.'

'What if Mam wants me to mind the kids?'

'Well, you can go to the house, but not to the shops. Have you got that?'

During that day I noticed my mam was really, really bad. She didn't want to walk, and was obviously in pain. And by the end of the day she had to go into hospital. It turned out to be the beginning of diabetes.

Stephen and myself were staying with Stephen's mam, Lily, in Ballymun. So I arrived back in Ballymun with Stephen and a suitcase and my little sisters to mind. Everybody thought I had had these kids before I got married.

There were a couple of old dears saying, 'I knew it! I knew it! Marrying a girl with two kids and him not even the father!' It was Margaret and Bridget I minded. And then I ended up with Debbie and Lisa, so I'd got two babies and two toddlers running around, because Mam was kept in hospital. I always kept contact with my family, and I often minded the kids. As the little kids started getting older, they called me a snob.

They said it in a jokey way. It was because I've always been well organized and they are so laid-back.

After the wedding we hadn't any money left. Literally none. I think we had three pounds between us. It was strange. We had no money. We had no place of our own. But I've never been so happy.

When we'd saved a bit of money, we got a flat of our own. We promised each other we'd work as hard as we could to build a better life. In the meantime I discovered I was pregnant. I couldn't believe it. I had no symptoms. Nothing. It turned out I was five months pregnant. That meant I'd been pregnant when we married, but I'd had no indication of it at all.

I stopped drinking the day I discovered, and I asked the doctors to take me off my medication. I was terrified the pills would harm the baby. A couple of weeks later, when I was five and a half months pregnant, I started feeling these pains. I knew something wasn't right. I went into the hospital; they gave me a scan, and told me I'd just had a miscarriage.

They were taking the probe off my tummy, and they were about to bring me up to the theatre, when suddenly a nurse stood stock still.

'Be quiet, everyone,' she said. Then she left the room at a run. She said she was going to fetch the doctor. She seemed to take such a long time. I was distraught. I was hanging on to Stephen's hand for dear life. I remember my mam was waiting outside. Finally the doctor came in, and told everyone to be really, really quiet. And then a miracle happened. We could hear this heartbeat. It was faint, very faint, but it was definitely there. Everyone in the room looked mystified.

'I don't understand,' I said. 'Does that mean I didn't have a miscarriage?'

The doctor didn't answer. Instead he asked, 'Are there twins in the family?'

'Yes.' I couldn't understand why he was asking me that. 'Yes, there are. On my dad's side of the family. So, have I not had a miscarriage?'

The doctor sat beside me and took my hand. 'Patricia, you have had a miscarriage. I'm sorry.' I was sobbing. 'But you are still pregnant.'

'I don't understand.'

'You were pregnant with twins.'

'I was?'

'But I'm afraid one of the twins died inside you. Maybe at just two and a half months.'

'But why? Why would that happen?'

'Sometimes it just does. Probably it wasn't getting enough nourishment.'

'What about the other baby?'

'The other baby is fine.' They brought me straight up to the ward and put me on a drip. After that the pregnancy went well. Our son, Stephen, was born on 1 August 1981.

We were over the moon. And, now that we were a proper family, we made a pledge to each other. We decided we were going to work very, very hard.

'And, Trish, I am never ever going to lie to you about money.'

'About money?'

'About borrowing. Or anything else. I know your parents had a tough time, and mine weren't perfect either. We're not going to be like that. Not ever. You can trust me, and I know I can trust you.'

I nodded. 'You mean because we both know how much trouble you can get into when you lie?'

'Exactly.'

Stephen was working night shifts. It was hard for me, managing the night feeds without him. But it was necessary. At that time, I sometimes felt the angels around me, but I always told them to go away. I was still scared about being sent back to hospital. And I never told Stephen about the angels. Not a whisper. If I told him about the spirit world, I was scared he would think I was mad and would leave.

Then, just before Christmas of the following year, Stephen got made redundant. I was expecting our second child by then. He came home with the redundancy cheque, and we sat there, in our tiny little flat in Ballymun, trying to decide what we could do. The cheque wasn't for very much. Stephen looked out of the window. He was thoughtful.

'There must be something out there I can do,' he said. 'There simply must be. Because, whatever else, I'm *not* going on the dole.'

I really respected him for that. He's a good, hard-working man. And he's a very proud man too.

In my head I said, *Angels, if you are still there with me, and I know you are, please help Stephen. Please guide him.*

I felt guilty asking them for something when I wasn't talking to them any more, but they didn't let me down. Within a day, Stephen had come up with an idea. He came back one evening, all excited.

He said, 'I have it, Trish. I have it. I know exactly what it is I should do.'

I looked at him then, wondering if he was going to share his big idea with me. Then he did.

'Newspapers.'

I started laughing. 'Newspapers?'

'How many shops are here in Ballymun?'

'I don't know. I never counted them.' I think I was being

sarcastic. There I was, with one baby, pregnant with a second, and no job. And I hadn't a clue what he was on about.

'We can use the redundancy money to set up a newspaper round.' And he did. He successfully ran that for many years, building it up into a great business. He did so well that we were able to save extra money to put away for our children. It wasn't easy. Stephen worked all the hours God sends. And all this time, I was on and off antidepressants; and not just antidepressants either. I also took Valium on and off to help my nerves and I was on sleeping tablets.

When Alan had been born, Archangel Michael came again. I knew he'd been there all the time. He would tell me he was giving me strength and courage, but what he was really doing was scaring me. I didn't want to see him, because that would mean I was mad. Or that others thought I was mad. So I'd go down to the doctor, and tell him I wasn't feeling the best. He'd give me the tablets, and I'd stop seeing the angels again. I felt that was the right way to go. I felt it was the only way.

I had so much to lose, now that I was a mother. I was really frightened I would be taken away – and this time that would mean I'd have to leave my children. I felt complete and utter fear. Then, when I stopped seeing the angels, I'd want to come off the pills again. I'd say I was feeling fine, and they'd gradually take me off them again. Then I wouldn't be long off, and I'd see the angels again. I'd try and fight it. Of course I would. I'd be saying, 'I'm not seeing youse angels; I'm not seeing youse,' but they'd get stronger with me.

And the truth is, when they were with me I felt really happy. I felt that things were crystal clear with me. But I hadn't the confidence to stay off the pills. The fear was too much. So I'd go back to the doctor. This went on for years and years.

I had decided after my second son was born that it wasn't right to have another baby. We were lucky to have the two boys, but we were struggling. It would be worse if we had more children. For the first time ever, I went and asked the doctor for the Pill. I felt kind of stupid, because I didn't know anything about the Pill. I was actually naive. He knew that I had two little boys born within a year of each other.

'I really couldn't cope with another baby. Not right now. I mean not financially.' I blushed. I hated explaining our affairs to him. But he was nice. He didn't hesitate to write me out a prescription.

'Here you are.' He handed it over the desk to me. 'Take one pill every day.' And I did. But a few weeks later I got a kidney infection, so I was back in to see the doctor. This time he gave me a prescription for antibiotics. I'd finished the course, but one evening after I'd settled the boys down for the night, I didn't feel too well. Stephen was home and we were talking away. I told him.

'It could still be the kidney infection,' he said. 'That gave you pain, didn't it? Maybe the antibiotics didn't work. They don't always.' But the pain wasn't the same. And it was getting stronger and stronger and stronger in my tummy.

'No, Stephen. It's something else. I'm scared.' We hadn't a phone in our little flat, so Stephen went over to the shopping centre to ring a doctor. My regular GP wasn't on duty, so a call-out doctor came. He examined me, prodding my tummy. I remember his hands were cold. He was quiet all the time he was examining me. When he was finished he looked up.

'Could you be pregnant?'

'No, no! I couldn't be. I'm on the Pill.' I explained about the kidney infection, and asked him if that could be the cause.

'Were you on antibiotics for that?' I nodded. He looked glum, and called Stephen.

'I want your wife to go into hospital straight away.'

So Stephen said, 'Can you give me a few minutes? I have to go and fetch Mam to mind the boys.'

He didn't take long. She only lived down the road. They took me into the Rotunda and ran a scan. The doctors there were really nice.

They said to Stephen, 'She has an ectopic pregnancy.'

That meant that I was pregnant, like the doctor had said, but the baby was growing in my tube. I couldn't believe it.

'I can't be pregnant. I'm on the Pill.'

'But I understand you've just finished a course of antibiotics?'

I nodded.

'Sometimes they interfere with the Pill.'

Nobody had warned me about that.

'We must operate within twenty-four hours.'

They gave us the picture from the scan.

All I could see was this little dot. 'So that's the baby?'

The nurse smiled and nodded.

They operated on me the next morning. They opened me from hip to hip. When I woke up, a good few hours after the operation, they had my legs kind of pinned up. I was really upset. I was in an awful lot of pain, but what really upset me was the thought of the baby gone.

When the doctor heard I was awake, he came and sat by the side of my bed.

'How are you feeling, Mrs Buckley?' he asked.

'Very sore.'

'Yes. I'm sure you are. And you will be, I'm afraid, for quite a time.'

'Is the baby gone?'

He nodded. Then said, 'But we didn't find the foetus. It was odd. We looked for it everywhere.' I just accepted that. I hadn't any choice. They kept me in the Rotunda for ten days. On the day I was leaving, the nurse came and asked for a urine sample.

'We want to check that there's no infection,' she said. 'If there is, we'll put a prescription in the post to you. So if you don't get a prescription, that means you don't have an infection.'

'OK. I understand.'

She handed me an appointment card. 'We want to see you in six weeks' time. Is that OK? Just to check the scar and see how you're doing.'

We went home, and I struggled to look after the boys. I found it difficult. It was hard lifting them with this big scar. It was really painful. I didn't get a prescription, so I figured there couldn't have been an infection there.

Stephen drove me to the Rotunda for my six-week check-up.

'There's no point in you coming in,' I said. 'This is only a check-up, and I shouldn't be long. You might as well wait in the van.' I checked in with the nurses, and it wasn't long before I was called into the surgeon's office.

'How are you?' he asked, peering at me over his glasses.

'A bit better, thanks. The soreness is starting to go away now.'

'Good. I'd better take a look at that scar,' he said, motioning me over to the couch. 'That's good,' he said. 'That's healing up nicely.'

'It is?' I was glad he thought so. Because if you asked me it looked terrible! All pink and ridged.

'And it will take a while to heal completely. You know that, don't you?' I nodded. 'Well, then, there's just one thing left to say.' I looked at him blankly. 'Congratulations!'

'Sorry?'

'Congratulations, Mrs Buckley.'

This was really confusing. 'Congratulations for what?'

'You're pregnant.'

Was he completely mad?

'I can't be. I can't be pregnant.'

He laughed. 'What I mean is, you're *still* pregnant. We took a test the day you left the hospital.'

'Yes. I remember. But that was to check for an infection.'

'Which there wasn't. But while we were about it, we did a pregnancy test too. And it was positive.' I was looking at him with my mouth hanging open.

'But how? How could I be still pregnant? You mean the baby is still in my tube?'

He shook his head and explained that the baby must have slipped down during the operation. He said that the only place they hadn't checked was my womb. He asked me was I pleased, but I couldn't take it in. I ran out of the hospital screaming. I had awful visions in my head. I was imagining the baby would be born with no arms and legs.

I ran past the van. Poor Stephen had to chase me. I was halfway up O'Connell Street before he caught up with me. He calmed me down and came back into the Rotunda with me. He made such a fuss. He was furious with the doctor for scaring me like that.

He said, 'Look at her! She's in such a state.' So we saw the doctor again, and they gave me a scan to show me that everything was OK.

'You see, Mrs Buckley,' said the doctor when they'd done the scan and I'd heard the heartbeat, 'you don't have to worry.

The baby will be fine. Yes, that was a bad start, but it's all fine now.'

Stephen was reassured, but I was still terribly upset. I was thinking, *How is this going to be OK?* I couldn't get my head around it. It all seemed so unlikely, after I'd had such a big, big operation.

The doctors kept a very close eye on me. When I was four months pregnant I got really bad morning sickness. I couldn't keep anything down, so they brought me into hospital and put me on a drip. That stopped me getting dehydrated.

It was terrible. I found that really hard. I wanted to be with my two boys at home. Stephen was quite amazing. He did a fantastic job. His mam looked after the boys so that he could work. He still had the newspaper round. He'd be out early and be finished by ten in the morning. He'd look after the boys for the day, and then go back out to do the evening run. Then he'd come in and visit me, and then go home again. It was so good to see him every day. He was great at trying to console me.

By the time I got out of hospital, I was almost five months pregnant. I was fine for a while. Fine except for the soreness from the scar. The doctors were a bit worried about the pressure on the scar from my pregnancy. There was pressure on the scar both from the outside and the inside.

When I went in for my six-month check-up, they found another problem. They had trouble finding the baby's heartbeat, and said the beat had got really low. That scared me so much. They took me back into hospital, and they kept monitoring the heartbeat. It kept going low. But when I was seven months pregnant, the doctors began to relax. Everything seemed fine. This was July 1984. I asked the doctors was it OK if I went home.

'I'm feeling much better now.'

'You can go – if you promise not to do too much. I know that will be hard for you, with your children. But make sure that husband of yours does the hard work. Is that understood?' I nodded.

I was really excited when Stephen came to collect me. It felt wonderful to be wearing clothes again, having been sitting around in my nightie. But as I walked out of the hospital that day, I had a strange feeling. I felt sure that something was wrong. I clutched Stephen's arm.

'Stephen, let's go and see Granddad Tommy.'

'No, Trish. We'll not go. We need to get you home so you can rest.'

'But . . .'

'That's what you promised the doctors.'

'Oh, OK.' Even as I said that, something was niggling at me. Granddad Tommy was on my mind constantly. But we went home. The boys were delighted to see me. They clambered all over my lap – even though Stephen told them to be careful. We played with them for a while, then read them a story and got them settled for the night.

At ten that night there was a knock on our door. Stephen went down to open it. I could hear him talking and then I heard it was the guards. I thought, *Stephen is after getting a parking ticket, and he doesn't want me to know because he thinks it will upset me.* I'll never forget his face when he walked in to me.

He said, 'Patricia, I have something to tell you.'

And I looked into his eyes and said, 'Stephen, it's OK. It's only a parking ticket.'

'Oh, Trisha. I wish it was.' I knew then something was *really* wrong. Stephen put his arm round me. 'I don't want you to get upset.'

'What is it?'

'I'm really sorry, Trish. Granddad Tommy passed away today.'

'I knew it. I knew we should have gone to see him. What time?'

'Sometime during the afternoon.'

'Oh.' I put my hands to my face. 'I wish we'd gone.'

'Trish, you weren't to know.'

'But I knew. I had this really bad feeling.'

I hadn't told Stephen about the spirit world. So when something like that happened, he would always ask, 'How did you know that?'

And I'd just say, 'I don't know. I don't know. I just had this strange kind of feeling.'

And he'd say, 'Oh, Trish! You and your feelings.'

Granddad wasn't ill. He hadn't been sick. He got up that morning and went to Mass. And that was something he never did.

Nanny Chris had looked up and said, 'You're not going to Mass, Tommy Carroll. I know you. You're going down the pub.'

He said, 'I'm not.'

But Nanny Chris could not understand why he would go to Mass. He'd only go if there was a wedding or a funeral. He wasn't like my other granddad, who went to Mass every day. But it was like, that particular morning, something told him to go.

He came home after Mass and was having a laugh and a joke with Nan.

He said, 'Ah, you'd want to see the old biddies down there.' She started slagging him. And he said, 'Chris, I think I'll just have a lie-down on the sofa.'

She had the dinner on. There were just the two of them in the house. And when the dinner was ready, she called him. But he was sound asleep, and he didn't wake up. She didn't try hard to wake him. She put his dinner on a plate, and over a pot to keep warm, and she had her own dinner.

While she ate, she was saying, 'Tommy, this dinner is lovely. And you needn't think I'm going to keep it boiling long for you.'

She didn't worry. Not for a while. But later she could not wake him. It was seven o'clock that night when she called into a neighbour and said, 'I can't wake Tommy.'

It turned out that he had been dead for a while. Nanny Chrissie never forgave herself, but there was nothing she could have done. He just lay down and went to sleep and never woke up.

It was so sad for her – for Nanny Chris. She and Grand-dad Tommy had a great relationship. They were both very modern in their outlook. They'd been married so long and they still held hands. They were still so much in love.

Nan didn't want me to know about Granddad. She knew I'd just got out of hospital that day, and she knew I was supposed to be resting. She was terrified something would happen to me, and she knew all the problems I'd already had in the pregnancy. When we got the call that night, we got Stephen's mam in, and we went straight over to Nanny Chris. Of course we did. But she got more upset about me, almost, than she was about herself. Her mind couldn't focus on Granddad.

She was saying, 'He wouldn't want you getting upset.'

I was seven months pregnant. It didn't add up for me. Granddad Tommy was so positive about my pregnancy. He kept telling me that he knew the baby would be OK. He was convinced of it. And he felt sure I was going to have a girl, too. A girl called Kym Louise.

He'd say, 'Kym Louise will come into the world, and she will be fine.' I couldn't believe that he would not be alive to see her.

Granddad Tommy was buried on 1 August 1984. That was Stephen's third birthday. Getting through the funeral was really hard. It was hard for all of us.

I went into labour on 17 September. I was over eight months pregnant. It was a Monday night, and I was at home. I went into hospital, but when I arrived there, my waters had not yet broken. It was a long labour. Kym Louise wasn't born until Wednesday afternoon at two minutes past five. And when she was – finally – born, when they handed her to me, I kept counting her fingers and her toes. I just couldn't let her go. She was perfect. And I had been so terrified that she would not be. I had been frightened the whole way through my pregnancy. I was terrified, but at the same time I would have accepted her if something had been wrong.

I'd made friends with all the nurses from the antenatal ward, because I'd been in so much. And when they heard I'd had my baby, they all came up to the postnatal ward, and said, 'Where is Kym Louise? We have to see Kym Louise.' They all came in, because they all knew the long saga: that I'd had the operation for the ectopic pregnancy, and then the pregnancy survived. They were so thrilled to see her. They passed her around, and they all said she was beautiful. But then, she was.

13 Waking Up

I didn't talk to the angels, but I was aware of them
around me.

Now that we had three children, we decided to put our names
down for a house. Our flat was so small, and it was on the
top floor. That had always been hard, but it was especially so
with three children. I've never liked using lifts, and bouncing
the children up and down the stairs was tough.

When we applied for the house, we didn't really expect to
get one. Or if we did get one, we thought we'd end up with
an old house. But we were lucky. When Kym was about nine
months old, the corporation gave us a house in Blanchardstown. It was on a new estate and there were a lot of young
couples moving in. We'd noticed the estate before; we'd
driven into it, and thought it looked really nice. But we really
didn't think we had a hope of getting in there.

They gave us a lovely four-bedroom corner house, and we
were delighted with it. The boys loved it. They adored the big
garden. Well, they did when they were used to it. I remember
the day we moved in, Stephen junior and Alan ran into the
house.

They were looking into every room, shouting, 'Ma, Ma.
Where's the balcony?'

They hadn't a clue. They didn't understand that the garden
was ours, and that they could play in it. We were very happy

in that house. There were lots of young couples with children, and that meant that our children had lots of friends to play with.

We still hadn't a lot of money. Stephen had his paper run, but it wasn't bringing in a lot of money because he was still building it up. He did get an extra job here and there and that helped. There was, anyway, always food on the table. We weren't extravagant at all. We couldn't afford to be. Everything we did was for the children.

It helped that Stephen was good with his hands. He'd make things out of wood. He made kitchen presses, and that all helped. I always said he was gifted in that way.

Kym was a year and a half old when I started feeling ill. It was terrible. I felt tired all the time, and I really didn't feel right. I thought at first it was just the strain of having three young children. I thought it was just because I was running around after them, and then there was the worry about money. That was always a pressure.

I got these really bad pains in my stomach. They were terrible, and they weren't getting any better. One day I couldn't take the pain any longer. I knew deep inside me that something was really wrong. I still wasn't communicating with angels at that stage, but I did have a sort of second sense. That was something that never left me.

I went to the doctor and explained it all to him. He took a cervical smear, and when the results came back, there were some 'abnormal' cells. So then he sent me to the Rotunda for a repeat test. They also did blood tests and a laparoscopy. Within two weeks they had the results back. They brought me in and sat me down, and said, 'I'm really sorry.'

'What?'

'We've found abnormalities. You're going to be fine. But there is only one thing we can do to make sure of that.'

'What's that?'

'I'm afraid we're going to have to perform a hysterectomy. You know what that means?'

'That you have to remove my womb?'

'Yes, Patricia. I'm afraid so. And that means no more children.'

I was devastated. I was twenty-six years of age. I thought, *No, this can't be happening*. At some stage I maybe would have liked another child.

I asked them, 'Surely there is something else you can do?'

'No. There is no choice. You have an early form of cancer. We've caught it very early, but without a hysterectomy you won't be here in two years' time.'

They took me into hospital. It was heartbreaking. I couldn't bear leaving my children. I had the hysterectomy and I wasn't feeling well afterwards at all. I remember feeling so lost, so empty. And I tried to get my head around this happening to me, especially so young. It's a strange feeling, you know; it was almost like I was a shell. That was how it seemed to me.

It took me a long time to recover from the operation. But I thought at least that would be the end of my problems. Unfortunately I was wrong. Just over two years later I started feeling unwell again. I was sent back to the Rotunda. I was twenty-nine. They said I had to have my ovaries removed. That was another big operation. I found the whole idea of it terrible.

During the operation, something very strange happened. I could see myself lying on the operating table. I was hovering above my body. I could hear the doctors, and I could see that I was losing a lot of blood. There seemed to be panic in the theatre. Then I turned, and I could see a very long hallway. At the end of that hallway there was a very bright light. And bathed in that light I saw Nan and Granddad. I started to walk towards my grandmother. Just to see her again was so wonderful. As I walked towards her, she held her arms out to me. And just as I got to her, my hands barely tipped hers, and I remember thinking, *It's been such a long time since I've seen you*. And I wanted to go with her. I really wanted to. And I saw lots and lots of angels all around. I thought, *They are back*.

They said, 'We never left you, Patricia. And you are welcome back to us.'

As I was about to walk through the tunnel door and move to the other side, Nan gently turned me round. She said, 'No, Patricia. You must go back. You must go back to your children. It's not your time to come to us.'

She told me I had lots of work to do.

'You have work to do with the angels. But it will be many years before you will do that work.'

I didn't understand what she was talking about. But I do remember it made me afraid.

'No, Nan. I can't work with the angels. I can't ever. If I do, they will lock me up again. You know they will.'

'No, Patricia. No, they won't. Because in many years' time you'll be fine. You'll see. You will have the strength.'

It was so good talking to Nan – because she understood about angels. I was so happy there, I really didn't want to go back. I told her so.

'Patricia, you must go back. You must think of your children.'

I knew she was right. So I started walking back towards

that operating theatre. I went back into my body which was still on the operating table.

When the doctors came to see me after the operation I told them what had happened. And they were quite surprised. The surgeon said, 'Well, we did have a little mishap in the theatre. But everything is now OK. And you won't, I promise, need another operation again. This time, we really have fixed you. Everything is going to be OK.'

I still couldn't get that picture out of my mind. That picture of walking through that tunnel. Of seeing Nan. Seeing Granddad. And, most importantly of all, seeing the angels. It did make me think.

I told Stephen about it – just a mumbled version during those first days after the operation. But I don't think he took it in. He thought I was just rambling because of the morphine I was on to stop the pain. He thought that was making me doolally. Besides, he was just so relieved that I was alive. He told me he'd really thought I was gone. And I could see the worry and the relief in his face.

I never mentioned it again. I'd never told Stephen about the angels. Never. I was worried he would think I was mad. Even though I would say little things now and again, and he would look at me and think, *Why did she say that?* I still never told him.

Life went on for us all. We both worked hard. Then we got the opportunity one day to take over a small grocery shop in Cappagh Road, Finglas. Stephen had heard about it, but first we had to go and meet the landlady. Stephen and I went there together, and to our delight, she agreed to let us take it over. We hadn't really a clue how to run it. We'd never run a shop in our lives, but we thought we'd give it a go. And we did.

It was nothing to brag about, just a small portacabin, but we worked hard and we worked long hours. We kept that shop open seven days a week, for fourteen years, and we did well. We did so well that we were able to save, and we bought our house off the corporation.

Then we decided to move. We'd loved that house. It had been a wonderful place for us, but it had always been our dream to move to the country. We'd just never had the money to do that. I would have liked to do it when the children were still young. By the time we made the move, in 1996, they were teenagers.

We managed to sell our house, and we bought this small, run-down cottage in the country, in County Meath. It takes about forty minutes to get in to the shop. The nearest shop to me is four miles away. The cottage is on a country road and there's a house a mile further on. I look out at thirty-five acres of farmland towards Pudding Hill. I can see the Cooley Mountains. It's really gorgeous.

When we moved in, the first thing I noticed was the peace. The quiet. It was like being in heaven. The children, though, didn't see it like that. When we brought them up to show them the house, we were saying, 'It's not that far. It's only a short drive.' But what did we do? We took a wrong turn and ended up driving for an hour. Of course there was nothing there. Just fields. They didn't like it, and it did take them time to settle in, but they did eventually.

We had our grocery shop still. Our landlady lived next door to the shop. She was a lovely lady called Mrs Lynch. And I mean a lady. She used to talk about Kilmoon, in County Meath. She'd go on and on about it. Our little cottage wasn't far from there. I remember telling her about it. She'd ramble on and ask me about the markets up there, but I hadn't seen any markets.

After a while, we had a problem with mice in the shop. We needed to call pest control. The girl who came out turned out to be Mrs Lynch's granddaughter. She came in and Stephen offered her a cup of tea or coffee.

'I'd love a coffee. I've been on my feet all day. And then I'll get to work on your little problem.' She asked where we were living. 'Are you still in Blanchardstown?'

'No. We moved from there. We've got this lovely cottage up in Kilmoon.'

'Kilmoon? I know it. Where, exactly, are you living?'

We told her. And she said, 'I don't believe it! That's the place!'

'What place?'

'Where I used to live. I lived in your very cottage when I was a child. I was there with my parents.'

I felt we'd met that girl for a reason. Were it not for her grandmother, our landlady, we would not have been able to rent our shop. And without the shop, we'd not have had the extra money to buy the cottage. To me, that was the angels' way of working with me and my family. Because they knew about our dream of moving to the country, and they knew what was best for me.

Not that I was talking to the angels. Not then. I would be aware of them around me sometimes, but I'd always tell them to go away. I'd tell them I couldn't see them. Even after all that time, I was still on and off antidepressants.

One day, I was serving in the grocery shop, and one of our regular customers came in. She was always a jolly lady, but this day she was really happy. I'd never seen her so happy. She was bouncing all over the place, and smiling broadly.

'What has you in such good form today?'

'I've just been to see my psychic medium.'

That was something I'd never thought of before. 'Never,' I said. 'Go away.' I asked her all about it, and she was so enthusiastic.

'It always makes me feel good, seeing her,' she said. And I could tell. She was really glowing with happiness.

'I'd love to go to one of them.' Stephen gave me a strange look then, because I'd never mentioned it before. I'd never even thought about it. In fact, I don't really know why I even said it. But I had.

So the customer said, 'Here, I'll give you the number.' She wrote it down on a piece of paper, and handed it over the counter. 'She's really good. You won't regret it, so you won't.'

It took me a few days to pluck up the courage to ring. And then, when I did, there was no answer. I was dialling that number for six whole weeks. Then, finally, somebody answered the phone. And when they did, it was strange.

They just said, 'Yeah!' in a bored kind of voice. A voice that made my heart sink. I thought, *I can't go and see someone who answers the phone like that*. It just didn't feel right. So I left it. It was a strong instinct. Or, as Stephen would have said, one of my feelings. I just felt that it wasn't meant to be.

14 Regaining Powers

I am home. I am back with my angels again.

The idea of a psychic stuck in my head. I'd never forgotten how happy the reading had made that customer. And one day, the free local paper came into the shop as usual. I picked it up, and was flicking through it when I found a big story about a lady who communicated with angels. I took the paper home, and as I read the story, I felt a connection with the lady. I felt, deep inside, that this was the lady I was meant to see. I asked my sister-in-law if she would come and have a reading too. She agreed, so I booked an appointment for the two of us.

The lady had a long waiting list. We had to wait six or seven weeks for an appointment, and during that time I was getting nervous. I didn't know whether I should go or not. Anyway, a few days before the appointment, the lady rang. She sounded lovely.

She had a beautiful gentle voice and she said, 'I have to cancel one of the appointments. I can only see one of youse.'

I said, 'I'll not go, then. I'll let my sister-in-law, Sandra, take the appointment.' I felt that she was keener than me. She wasn't as nervous. 'Sure, maybe you'll get me another appointment later.'

'No, no,' she said. 'It's you, Patricia, that I need to see.' She was definite about it. And I felt really, really terrible. I felt Sandra would be so disappointed.

Sandra worked for me in the shop now and again. When she came in that next afternoon, I told her what had happened. I told her the lady had insisted on seeing me and she said, 'That's fine. I don't mind. You go. Maybe she'll give me another appointment later.'

It was mid-November when I went for the reading. November 2002. And the night of the reading it was freezing cold. Stephen offered to drive me. It was in an estate in Blanchardstown and we hadn't a clue how to get there. We had to ring the lady again to get directions. And then we found it without much trouble.

I was really nervous that evening. I don't know what I was nervous of, but I was shaking when we pulled up at the house. Then I got such a strange, strange feeling over me. I could see angel lights around the house. Lights like I used to see before I stopped communicating with angels. That made me scared. I didn't want to get out of the car, but I felt a tiny little push. It felt strange, but I now realize it was the angels pushing me into the house. It was like they were saying, 'Go in. Go in.'

Stephen stayed in the car to wait for me. I felt bad about that, because the night really was bitter cold, and our car wasn't exactly new. It was a black Toyota Corolla. He put the heater on, but I'm not sure how effective it was. When I went in the lady greeted me. She was lovely, but there was nothing too different about her. She was an ordinary woman. She wore glasses and normal clothes; she was wearing trousers, I remember, and a blue blouse. She had a very gentle manner. I felt comfortable with her. She brought me into this little room where there were two chairs. There were lots of candles and the lights were turned down low. There was lovely, gentle music playing. She asked me had I ever been for a reading before and I said no.

'OK,' she said. But she was looking at me, and when she looked at me, I could see something whoosh past me. I was trying to sit very straight, but my eyes must have moved. I was thinking, *What was that!* The lady didn't comment.

'Well, just close your eyes for a second, and we will see what happens.' I closed my eyes. I remember my heart was beating really fast. And in my head I was saying, *Nanny . . . Granddad. If you are there, please talk to this lady. Please give her a message for me.*

And I was thinking that if they weren't there, maybe David – my cousin who died in his teens – would be, or perhaps Maria, another cousin who committed suicide at sixteen. I was saying, in my head, *One of youse – please give me a message, one of youse.* And as I was saying that in my head, I could feel something touching my face. I didn't say anything to the lady. I think I was worried she would think I was mad. I know that's silly, when she was doing this work, but I'd learned, through the years, to feel afraid. Anyway the lady started to speak.

'Do you live near a river?'

'No. I don't.'

'OK, then. Is there water near you?'

'No, there isn't.' I got a bit scared then. It was like she was seeing an accident about to happen.

Then she said, 'Do you have one brother?'

'No, I've got two brothers.'

She looked puzzled. 'Oh, OK. Right, fine.'

I thought maybe I was making things worse. So I opened my eyes, and her eyes were closed. And when I opened my eyes, I saw, right behind her, there were two huge wings. And I went, 'Ohhhh . . .'

'Are you OK?'

'Yes.'

'You're seeing something. I know you are.'

'No, I'm not.' I was terrified. I kept thinking, *Don't do that again. Don't give in to seeing angels.*

Then she said, 'I have a young boy here.' And she gave me his name. I was in complete and utter shock. I didn't really know the little boy who came through, but he'd passed away a couple of years previously, and he was only twelve years old when he died.

Although I hadn't known the boy, Stephen knew the family well. They'd been neighbours of his in Ballymun, and I knew them in passing, just to say hello and goodbye to. We hadn't seen them for a few years before their son passed away. A customer had told us about the accident. Stephen, who grew up with the boy's mam, was horrified, and I felt an urge to help them too. He knew where they lived, and we went over. We rallied round, and we helped them to organize the funeral. We minded her two smaller children for her, and we ended up driving them to the morgue. I remember holding the child's football in my lap. I guess the little boy really wanted the message brought back, and kind of knew I would do it.

I can tell you, I was shaking from head to toe. I was there for two hours, and it was all for this message from the boy. She gave me details of the boy and said the message had to be to his mam.

'It's for her ears only. You're not to tell anyone else. Not Stephen. Not anybody.'

I thought, *How am I going to do this?* I hardly knew this woman. I knew Stephen knew her family, but I wondered how I could tell a mother that I went to see someone who communicates with angels, and her little boy came through from the spirit world. To me.

'Do I have to?'

'Yes. You do.'

I was really disappointed that none of my family had come through. All I could do was take in everything she told me about the boy; all these details about his family. It was such a complicated message. And poor Stephen. All that time he'd been sitting in the car. He was absolutely freezing by this time.

He said, 'I think the guards thought I was going to rob the house or something.'

'What?' I was feeling in a daze after all I'd heard.

'Sure I've been here for so long,' he said. 'And a gardaí car has been driving up and down. Someone must have seen me sitting here and have called them.'

As we were driving out of the estate he turned to me and said, 'Well?' And I just burst into tears. I cried and cried and cried. I found I couldn't stop. I began to explain to him, about the lady and the room, and how she'd asked me to close my eyes. It came out in a rush. But then I stopped talking. It upset me to go on. Eventually he pulled the car over and gave me a hug.

'Are you OK?'

'Not really.' I was still shaking. 'You'll never guess who came through.'

'Your nan?' Stephen knew how I'd hoped she'd get in touch with me.

'No. No, it wasn't her.'

'Your granddad, then?'

'No. They didn't come. Neither of them came. Stephen, it was that boy who drowned.' There was a shock on Stephen's face. When we got home I told him I had a message for the little boy's mam and I was not to tell what the message was; it was for his mam and only his mam.

'Well, Trish, if that's what you've got to do, that's what you've got to do. You have to give the message to his mam.'

I was taken aback by that. Stephen never thought of the spirit world or angels or anything like that.

I was absolutely terrified. I waited a couple of days. I really didn't want to do it, but at the same time I felt this urge. I now know it was the angels saying, 'Please pass this message on.'

The message was very, very detailed. Part of the message was that when I knocked at his mam's door I wasn't to go into the house. He'd been really specific about that. Not until the message was passed on. We went on a Saturday. Stephen knew how nervous I was, so he came up with a brainwave.

'I'm going to buy a Dictaphone,' he said. 'Then you can record the message as it was said, and simply hand it over.'

We tested the Dictaphone outside the shop and it worked fine, but when we tried to use it on the way to the house it would not work. We got to the house and tested the Dictaphone out. It worked. But when I tried to record the message, it wouldn't work for me. It was as if the angels were saying, 'We don't want this recorded.'

I waited in the car, and Stephen went to the door. The boy's daddy opened the door. Stephen explained that I'd been to see a lady who communicated with angels. He explained what had happened. The man invited Stephen in, but he said no, and waited for the boy's mam. He beckoned to me, and I joined him on the doorstep.

She came down then. I expected her to go mad. But she didn't. She simply asked me in.

'I can't,' I said. 'I'm not allowed.' She raised her eyebrows when I said that. 'I can't see inside until I've given you the message.'

She nodded, and went to fetch her coat. It was really cold and we started walking. I didn't know where I was walking to. But as we were walking I was telling her the message.

'I don't know if this message is right or not,' I said. But it all made sense to her. All the details he'd given me were accurate. She confirmed everything. There were some very personal messages for her. She was very moved by all she heard.

Then I stopped walking. I just stopped dead, and she asked me why.

'I don't know. I just had a strange urge to stop there.' And she gave me a hug. I was surprised. 'What was that for?'

'Turn around and look over there.' And when I did, I could see the graveyard that the boy was buried in. And it's where she would have walked most days. It was also the spot where the boy used to play.

She said, 'Thank you for passing the message on to me.'

As we walked back she looked more peaceful. It was as if a weight had been lifted from her. I felt that she'd needed to hear from her son. And she'd needed to hear from him that day. When we got back to her house, she said, 'Now, come in for a cup of tea. Please come in.' And I did. Then I realized why I hadn't been allowed in the house before. There were things in the sitting room the boy had been talking about in the message. There was a kind of altar to him, and his football boots were there. They'd been dipped in bronze, just like he'd told me in the message. She showed me the boots, exactly where he had said.

'How did you know?'

'It wasn't me,' I explained. 'It was the other lady. I just happened to go for a reading.'

When we were leaving, they walked us to the door. I was about to walk past one of the cars that was in the driveway, when I heard this little voice. It said, 'You've forgotten one thing.'

I stopped, and Stephen turned.

'Are you OK? You've gone really white.'

'I don't know if I'm OK.' I felt everyone was looking at me and I was terrified – maybe I had heard this wrong. The voice had said, 'Please don't forget the little buttercup.' Then I remembered, and I said, 'Right. Just one minute.' I bent down to look under the car, all the time thinking this must be wrong. How could there be a flower when this was all concrete? I had to get under the car. I lay down on my back like a mechanic, thinking, *You'd just better be right.* I put my hand under and I was feeling around, and I just plucked it. Out came the yellow buttercup and I handed it to his mam.

'This is for you from your son,' I said. She just started crying.

I felt better once I'd passed the message on. Going home I felt really happy. I felt if I hadn't passed the message on, the spirit world would not have been very pleased with me. I believe it was the angels saying, 'Please trust us.'

At that stage, I still wasn't sure about the angels. I had started to see little things, but I'd say no. It was all very well giving that message. It felt good, but the disappointment was still there too.

I thought, *Nanny and Granddad mustn't be talking to me.*

Anyway, I went back to work, and a couple of evenings

later the lady from Blanchardstown rang me. She said, 'I really need to see you.'

'Why?' I was puzzled.

'The spirit world is telling me I need to see you.'

'But I did what you said. I passed that message on. And the boy's mammy and daddy said thank you.'

'No, it's not that. I need to see you again. Will you come?'

I agreed, but this time I asked Stephen to go in with me, and he said he would. I think he was a bit mystified, to be honest. I don't think he had a clue what was going on. He brought me just to keep me happy. We both went in, and Stephen talked to the woman's husband in the kitchen while she brought me back to the little room.

'Thank you, Patricia, for passing that message on.'

'That's fine. Thank you for allowing me.'

'Do you know, Patricia, I've not been able to do any work.'

'God, I'm so sorry. Were you ill?'

'Nope. But now I have a message for you.' She smiled then. 'Patricia, your nan's here.' I gave a great sigh of relief. It was lovely when she gave me the messages from Nan. First she described her to me. She said she had a leg amputated. 'I'm sorry you didn't get the message from her first, but this was just the way it was meant to be.' Then she opened her eyes. 'Your grandmother did this work?'

'Yes, she did. She communicated with the spirit world.'

'Patricia, your nan says that you are not going to suffer spiritually any more.'

'I don't understand.'

'You have suffered spiritually for very many years. You've locked it away. Well, now the angels are unlocking it. Patricia, the angels are all around you. They tell me you used to talk to them.' I began to feel anxious, but she said, 'They've said to tell you that you're not mad.' I sat there and I looked at her. Then I started to cry. She came over and gave me a hug.

'Are you OK?'

'I am. It's just to hear those words, "You are not mad." And to hear that the angels are with me again.'

'Patricia, they never left you. Do you understand? They never ever left you.' She smiled then, and took my hands in hers. 'They are very sorry about everything you had to go through because of your beliefs and your dedication to the angels.'

'They are?'

'And you're to go home and set up an angel altar.'

'An angel altar?'

'Yes. There's work for you to do.'

'I don't know if I can.'

'Patricia, they want you back. They wouldn't let me work until I told you that.'

I was mystified, but I said I would.

The reading was over, but we stayed in that room. We chatted and chatted. We talked about angels. It was the first time, for so many years, that I'd been able to talk about them. She explained then that the angels had told her, before that first time, that they wanted me to be alone for my appointment. They told her it would all take a lot of time.

I found all that a bit strange; but it put me on top of the world. It was so wonderful to talk to someone who believed in what I believed in. And even though I hadn't communicated with the angels for so many years, I felt this very strong urge. I felt, *I am home. I am back with my angels again.*

The lady could see my relief.

'If you need help, Patricia, all you have to do is lift the phone. I will give you any help you need.'

'Thank you.' I couldn't think what she meant. Why would I need help?

'Patricia, you will work with angels. They will be communicating with you. All you have to do is answer them when they talk to you.'

15 Healing

Archangel Michael gives strength and courage. He
helped me cut the links with the past.

On the way home I was quiet. I thought, *How am I going to
explain this one?* When we arrived home Stephen remarked
on it.

'You're very quiet,' he said.

'I'm just taking in what the lady said to me. She said to put
up an angel altar.'

He said, 'All right. But where do you get angels from?'

'I just don't know. Anywhere I've been I've never seen an
angel figurine.'

'And where will you put it – this altar?'

'I could use the spare room. If you don't mind?' Stephen
agreed. But I decided not to set it up until after Christmas.

Meanwhile, Stephen had had an idea for a Christmas
present for me. He wanted to give me an angel for my altar,
but he wasn't sure where he could get one. He went on to
the web, and came across a place in Iceland that sells angels.
They were handcrafted. Come December, they hadn't
arrived, so he rang to inquire. It turned out they'd been
seized by the Customs at Dublin airport. Stephen rang
Customs again and again, but he didn't get anywhere. So
realizing that he most probably would not get the angels in
time for Christmas, off he went into Dublin and did a search.

He found a little gold angel in a jewellery shop. So he figured, *I'll get her that.*

I think it's very funny. I reckon the angels decided I was getting two angels that year, because on 24 December Stephen got a call from the Customs to say that his parcel was ready to be released. So I got both his angels on that Christmas Day.

We got over Christmas and I set up my altar and started, in my own way, talking now and again to the angels. And just waiting for something to happen. But meanwhile I was feeling better. Ever since I'd seen the lady I'd been less nervous. I'd cut back on my Valium. I didn't feel the need for it any more.

I was still seeing the psychiatrist, but each time I went back I was looking more and more myself. I was taking better care of myself too. I cared what I looked like, and I was wearing just a tiny bit of make-up. The psychiatrist was noticing a change. He asked me if something good had happened to me, but I just smiled. I wasn't going to tell him the reason. There was no way I would say I was feeling better because I was communicating with the angels. I thought, *I'll keep that bit to myself.*

Since the incident with Barry, I'd been terrible for wearing black. If we were going out anywhere I would wear a black skirt, or black trousers and a black top. It was always black. But around that time I bought a lilac top and two white blouses, and some clip-on tiny diamond earrings that brightened my face up. People were noticing. People were saying it, even in the grocery shop.

'Gosh, don't you look lovely today.'

The angels said it too. They said, 'You are brightening yourself up, and your energy is becoming brighter.'

Anyway, every time the psychiatrist gave me a prescription I collected it, but I never took the pills. So I started gathering all my tablets up. One morning I was lying in bed, and I was feeling a bit low. This was probably because I had come off the tablets without the help of the doctors. Stephen had gone to work, and Kym to college. I didn't bother going to work.

Stephen was used to that, used to me saying, 'I'm just not going in today.' Not that he liked it. He'd say his nerves were gone, having to leave me. At the back of his mind he thought I might do something to harm myself. I had never tried, and I never would, but that didn't stop Stephen worrying.

I could feel the presence of something, and when I opened my eyes, there was an angel at the end of the bed. It gave me such a shock. I lay back and put the duvet over my head.

'Go away,' I said. 'I'm not seeing you. I'm not seeing you.'

A couple of minutes later I took another peek and the angel said, 'I'm still here.'

I remember sitting up and looking at her. She was beautiful. There was a shimmering light around her and her hair was raw red. 'I'm Simone. I'm your guardian angel, and I'm not going away, Patricia. In fact, I never went away.'

I propped myself up in the bed. I was sitting there, talking to her, but in my head I was thinking, *Am I really talking to her?* I didn't say it out loud, but she said, 'You are. And we need a really long chat.'

'Well, in that case, I'm going to get a cup of tea.'

'But you'll come back?'

'Yeah. I'll make it, and bring it back in with me.'

So when I got out of bed, I was making myself a cup of tea, buzzing about. I was thinking, *I'll just load the dishwasher, and then I'll go back in and have a word with the angel.* I lifted my cup, and the next minute my spirit guide, Andrew, was standing there. I jumped.

'Jesus! Why do you do that to me?' He was so tall. So black. I had seen him on and off, over the years, but I'd always pretended he wasn't there. I kind of ignored him. He respected that I wasn't ready. That morning it was like a flash.

'Leave the dishwasher alone.'

'Why?'

'Just stop cleaning. Go back in.'

I laughed. 'I forgot how you boss me around. It's a pity you can't make yourself useful. It'd be great if you'd carry the tea back in for me.'

'That I can't do.'

Simone was still there, waiting for me. 'It doesn't have to be like this,' she said.

'But people will think I'm mad. It will be like it was before. Aren't I better off being like I am?'

'Now is your time to come back.'

'That's all very well. But how? How can I do that without being locked away again?'

'Patricia, I am only here to help you.'

'Help me?'

'Yes, you have got a lot of work to do. And we need you back on your path again.'

'But, Simone, I have to go to a psychiatrist. And when I do, I'll be given a load of tablets so that I don't see you any more.'

'But, Patricia, you don't need those tablets. You don't need them now and you never did need them.'

'What do you mean by that? I needed them when I had my breakdown. Surely I needed them then.'

'Back then, you were suffering from exhaustion. Nothing more. Exhaustion and grief.' I looked at her in astonishment. And I could believe what she said. Because when I'd slept for a few days in hospital I had begun to feel better. And it was only when I told the doctor about the angels that the harsher treatment started. I thought of all those wasted years, and I felt so sad.

'The spirit world needs to speak to you,' said Simone. 'There are people who need your help.' By now, Andrew had joined Simone at the end of my bed. I sat up in the bed, sipped my tea, and had a long chat with both of them.

'Andrew, are you going to get me into trouble?'

He just smiled at me. Ever the innocent. 'Would I do that? Patricia, my job is to help you. You've been away long enough now. It's time for you to come back. The spirit world is waiting. We're all lined up to talk to you.'

'That's all very well. But how do I tell my family this? How do I tell my husband?' Andrew and Simone just smiled. 'And what about my children? What about Stephen, Alan and Kym? How do I tell them that their mother is talking to people who are dead? Oh,' I shrugged, 'and also talking to the angels.'

'Don't worry.' Simone stroked me on the face, gently, with her wing. 'It will be fine. This time it's going to be fine.'

And I did feel better. Every day I was having communications with the angelic world. And with Andrew, my spirit guide. Archangel Michael, in particular, was absolutely brilliant to me. He said to me, 'I will give you the strength and the courage you need.'

He started introducing Archangel Raphael in those weeks when I was slowly coming off the tablets. Raphael was the healing angel. He would help me with the healing.

He would come into the room with me, and he told me to lie down and imagine the green light. Every time I did that, I felt so full of energy. The green was a healing balm. It would just hover above my body. It was like somebody placing a green silk sheet over my body. It was healing me emotionally. It was healing me physically. It was healing me mentally.

Archangel Michael was giving me strength and courage. He helped me cut the links with the past. He helped me to let go of all the hurt and the pain I had been through. He helped me to let go of the abuse that had happened. He allowed me to move on.

Then Archangel Gabriel came in. He was absolutely gorgeous. He was the one who helped me with my communication. I have to say I felt on top of the world, because I had all the angels around me. I had the archangels, I had Simone, my guardian angel, and I had Andrew, my spirit guide. I had them all every day helping me get stronger, psychically, mentally and emotionally.

I still hadn't told Stephen I was seeing angels again. I'd been putting it off. In February 2003 I decided it was time to tell the family. When Stephen came in from work, I told him I had something to show him, but that I wanted to wait until the whole family was there. So I waited until after dinner. During dinner Steve and the boys looked really worried. I realized they thought I was going to give them bad news. That made me feel guilty. I realized that was how they must often have felt when they were growing up with me – that any news was bound to be bad.

I went into the bedroom and came out with a brown Dunnes Stores bag. It was full.

I said to Stephen, 'Here you go.'

He said, 'What's this?'

'Take them. I don't need them any more.'

Stephen was slowly taking the bag off me but looking at me strangely at the same time. I remember him turning and looking at the children.

Kym said, 'What is it?' They could hear at this stage the rattle of the tablets.

Stephen opened the bag and said, 'What is this?' The shock on his face.

'It's all the tablets. Stephen, I don't need them. I haven't been taking my tablets – not for months. So please, either take them back to the chemist or burn them – I don't care – just get rid of them. I don't need them.'

We sat down and I explained to them. And I could tell Stephen was really, really nervous. Remember, ever since I had met Stephen I'd been on and off tablets. I told them all about the angel coming to me – about Simone.

'Simone told me I don't need the tablets any more. She told me I've never needed them.'

I think that came as a shock to them. They were so used to seeing me take tablets. When I told them I didn't need them, Stephen, in particular, found it really difficult to understand. They were worried about me. About the tablets. No wonder he felt so worried. I told him how the angels had been helping me. The family knew I had an angel altar. And they could see the difference in me. They could see I had a lot more energy.

Alan looked at me and then he looked at his dad and said, 'Oh Jesus! It's going to be the God squad.'

Everyone started laughing then. Alan is so funny. He's the family joker. You just don't know what he's going to come out with next. I know deep down he is spiritual, but he will say things like, 'That's mad. I don't believe in all of that.'

They asked me then what it was like. I found it difficult to explain it to them.

'It's like the old me has been washed away. It's like a new beginning. I can feel it in my soul.' I could feel this new brightness that I'd felt when I was a little girl. It was that same feeling when the angels were around me.

The eldest boy, Stephen, said, 'Mam, I always kind of knew there was something different about you.'

'Why did you just say that?'

'Because when we were growing up you used to say things that you shouldn't have known.'

'What do you mean?'

'I'd come in from school and you would say something like, "That was good, when you got full marks in the test" – something that had happened that day. I always used to wonder how my mam could have known that.'

I didn't remember saying that. I then started to tell them about seeing angels when I was younger. I told them what happened with the antidepressants, but they already knew that bit. They knew I'd had a bit of a breakdown and the doctors had said it was all in my head. They were very supportive then.

Stephen was thoughtful too. We'd been married for over twenty years by then, and he'd thought he knew everything about me.

He said, 'You know, I could never put my finger on it, but there were times, Patricia, when you would wake up and say you had this dream. You'd start telling me about it and suddenly stop. I'd encourage you to tell me, but you wouldn't. I never pushed you on it because I didn't want you to be upset. But there was always something about it.' He was very calm. Looking back now, I don't think there was ever a complete cut-off from the angels. They were always still around.

I remember, before all that happened, Stephen would be messing with me. He used to joke, 'I'm your guardian angel really.'

I used to stop and think, *If only you knew.* It's always been that bit of a joke and when everything came out, and I told him, he wasn't really so surprised. The family were so supportive. They then encouraged me so much – all of them. I'd thought, *My poor kids, they're going to think their mother's gone mad.* They didn't.

If I said something about the angels, they would just listen. And after that, Archangel Michael started coming in very strongly with me, and I'd say it to them. If they were going anywhere I'd say, 'Don't forget to ask Archangel Michael to come to mind you.'

They'd ask who he was, and I was able to explain to them. And they did start asking Archangel Michael to look after them if they were going on a night out. It became normal for them to do that. It was like the angels had always been here and never went away. And now the daughters-in-law, their families, everybody speaks to the angels. The boys might ring me and say, 'A friend is having a problem. Which angel should they talk to?'

The amount of encouragement that the children and Stephen gave me, I can't even describe. I stopped going to the psychiatrist then. I just never went back. I got letters from them about missed appointments, but I ignored the letters. I knew, now, that I didn't need to go back. I didn't need pills, or a psychiatrist. Not now that I was back with my angels. I have never ever been back. Not since 2003.

*

All of this was hard for Stephen and I knew he was worried. I couldn't really be surprised. All our married life I'd suffered from anxiety, and he'd always had to tiptoe round me, aware that I'd get these terrible feelings. And before, every time I'd tried coming off my tablets I'd been fine for a while, but had then got worse again. It had been a cycle, and how could he now believe that the cycle was broken?

I had never really known how he felt about it. I'd never understood until I came off the tablets for good and started to speak about the angels. It took me a long, long time to really explain that this hadn't just come out of the blue. The angels hadn't come to me on a whim. They weren't there just because I had been to see that lady in Blanchardstown.

It was difficult for both of us. I was starting a new lease of life. Before, I would have depended on medication to get me through the day. And now here I was, without medication, but with a new lease of life. I realized that Stephen probably expected my world to fall around me. I asked the angels to help. I asked Archangel Michael, because he spoke to me quite a lot.

I said, 'Archangel Michael, please can you help me to help Stephen to understand that my world is not going to fall down. And that I was on the path before, and fell off it, and now I'm back.'

This time I knew I was back for good. There is a lot more understanding now of the spirit world, and of guardian angels. And Archangel Michael did start to work on Stephen. But in his own way. Stephen is very good on computers. He thought it would be nice to set up a website, and to dedicate it to the angels. We hadn't a clue how to go about this, so we rang an internet company and asked for some help. The man said that first we had to find a name. We had a number of ideas, but we couldn't make up our minds. Stephen had to find out which names were available. Angels of Ireland was on our list. As Stephen was chatting the man said, 'Angels of Ireland sounds nice.' Stephen agreed it did. I think the angels were working with him to come up with that name. Anyway, we set up the site by March and called it 'Angels of Ireland'.

We still had the shop on the Cappagh Road, and we put some angel statues outside it. There was a really good response to them. We started to tell people about the website and we told them the name we had chosen.

Then one day a woman came into the shop and said she had seen our advertisement in the paper. We hadn't a clue what she was on about, but it turned out to be an advert that a woman called Mary K Hayden had placed in the paper. And lo and behold, the name of her company was 'Angels Ireland'. We rang Mary in a panic, thinking that she would think we had stolen the name from her, and just added the word 'of'. We explained that we hadn't meant to copy her name, and we hoped she didn't blame us. Mary just laughed.

'It doesn't matter at all,' she said. 'That is just the angels' way of bringing you and I together.'

Since that time we have become good friends with Mary, and with her husband, John. Mary sells meditation CDs which are some of the best and easiest I've ever come across. Meanwhile, I was still talking to the angels. My conversations with them were getting really clear. It was great to have them back with me.

It was great for my family too. They all noticed the change in me. How could they not? I was jolly in the mornings. I'd be really looking forward to the day. And before, I wouldn't. I dreaded my days, and there were a lot of days I never made it into work. I'd be feeling bad with no get-up-and-go. Now, with the angels, I was so happy. I was happy just to be alive.

By this time I had a little granddaughter, Rebecca. She was a year and a half by then, as she'd been born in October 2001. I loved her so much, but when I was on the medication playing with her would be exhausting. Now I had more energy I enjoyed her more. I felt happier and more alive.

16 Setting Up

We meet people for a reason. Often our paths are
meant to cross.

We had our website up and running. Everything was going
well, when one Saturday the modem broke. Stephen rang a
friend of his, Paul, who worked with computers, fixing them
and selling spare parts. He asked Paul if he had a modem.

'Could you not have rung earlier on? I'm after leaving the
shop now.'

'Well, sure,' Stephen said to him. 'If I'd known the modem
was going to break, I'd have let you know earlier.' They were
laughing about that, joking and bantering.

Anyway, Paul said, 'Look, it so happens I do have one. I'll
drop it up to the shop. Is that all right?'

'That's grand. See you in a while.'

When Paul arrived he said, 'Have you heard I'm moving
shop?'

'Oh God. No, I hadn't. Where are you moving to?'

'Not far. I'm moving down to the bottom of the hill.'

'What, in Finglas?'

'That's right. It's just a small shop, but it's grand.'

Stephen started messing with Paul. The two of them were
a bit mad, so they kind of slagged one another.

'Ah, will you rent us half the shop?' Stephen hadn't meant
to say that. And to this day, he doesn't know why he did.

'What?' Paul looked puzzled.

'Can we put a few angels in your shop?' We hadn't *got* any spare angels, so I don't know why he even said it.

Anyway, Paul didn't take him seriously. He just laughed and said, 'Angels and computer parts? Stephen, will you ever keep quiet for a moment.' Because, like I said before, Stephen never shuts up. 'Just stop and draw breath, will you? Because it so happens that the shop I'm renting is being split down the middle. It's too big for what I want.'

'Rent us the other half.'

'You're not serious?'

'Yes, I am.'

'I can't. It doesn't even belong to me.'

Stephen looked downcast. 'Look,' said Paul, 'I could introduce you to the landlord. If, that is, you really are serious?'

When Stephen told me all about the shop at the bottom of the hill, I was flabbergasted. We'd never even talked about owning an angel shop. We'd never discussed it. Yet he was really excited about it.

I didn't share his excitement. Not at first. I thought it was crazy. Why would I open an angel shop? Surely I didn't really know enough about angels. I didn't want to be a disappointment to anybody. But Stephen's enthusiasm was infectious. He kind of carried me along with him.

Anyway, Paul introduced us to Rory, the man who owned both shops. He came to see us at home and asked us what it was we were going to be selling.

'Hopefully, angels,' said Stephen. He was so sure it was a good idea. But I was still worried. What did I know about selling angels? All I knew was helping with papers and selling groceries.

'But you're talking to the angels, Trish,' said Stephen. 'So where's the problem?'

He didn't understand that because this was all so new – at least this phase was new – I was still very afraid.

The angels, though, agreed with Stephen.

'Patricia, please don't be afraid,' they said. 'This is what is meant for you. It's the start of your path.' They told me that Finglas needed an angel shop. 'Finglas needs light around it,' they said.

I was puzzled. 'How am I going to put light around Finglas? Or come to that, light around anywhere? I'm only back communicating with youse.' Then I had a terrifying thought. 'What if people think I'm mad?' After all, it wouldn't be the first time.

'They won't.' Simone, my guardian angel, came then and said, 'Trust us. Please trust us.'

Simone is absolutely wonderful. I do trust her. And she said to me, 'No harm is going to come to you ever again. Trust us.' So I did.

We opened the angel shop in June 2003. It was down the bottom of the hill, a tiny place. Stephen was in charge of the business side of things. He found out where to buy the stock from the internet.

When we first opened the shop I helped Stephen with the stock. He took me to a wholesaler in London who showed me some angels. I picked out the ones I liked. I've never had to help him again. He's very good at doing it himself. He says the angels are working with him too, and I believe that they are.

Stephen is very connected to the spirit world. He is always saying our paths were meant to cross. I do believe that. I'm a great believer in that.

We still had the grocery shop at this stage. Stephen ran that while I ran the angel shop. He'd come in sometimes to see how I was getting on. And people were coming in. It wasn't busy at first, but that quite suited me. It felt like a little hobby, and I liked that. But the angels had different ideas for me.

We were there for a couple of months, and I got to know some really nice people. There are some lovely people in Finglas. They'd keep coming back to the shop, and we'd chat. They began to confide in me. Some of them had happy stories, and some of them had really sad stories.

One day around September 2003, I was serving two ladies and chatting to them at the same time. Stephen had popped down and I asked him would he go to the shops and get me a sandwich. I hadn't taken a break and I was really hungry. When he'd gone, in walked this gentleman. He was an ordinary-looking man, maybe in his late fifties and probably on his way home from work. I remember he had a rucksack on. I was serving the two ladies, and with the man there too, the shop was getting crowded. That's how small it was.

As I was chatting to the ladies, I felt this sort of electric charge – this energy. I looked up, and the man was there, right in front of the counter. He had a moonstone in his hand. He'd picked it from our collection of little crystals.

'Hold out your hand.'

I gave him a look as if to say, 'Would you ever go away.' I was still serving the ladies.

'No, really. Hold out your hand.'

'No, I will not! Will you go away!' I was thinking, *Yeah, right!* I suppose that is a defence mechanism with me. I didn't know whether to laugh. I thought he was strange, but at the same time, I knew he was a good person. Andrew, my spirit guide, was there, towering over the man.

He said to me, 'Just do it. Trust him. Hold out your hand.' So I did. And this guy held out the moonstone. But he didn't immediately put it into my hand.

'Now. Close your eyes.' I was thinking, *What is this?* I really didn't want to close my eyes, but I sensed something special about the man. Meanwhile the two ladies were intrigued. They'd stopped talking to me, and were watching the man in absolute silence. We were all wondering what this was about. So I closed my eyes and he placed the crystal in my hand. Then he held my hand with his. Not tightly. He was very gentle.

The most amazing thing happened. I went straight back to 1974. And back to the Dublin bombings. I could see everything that had happened that day. I could see the child in the buggy, and I could see the buggy getting pushed away, but I couldn't see who was pushing it.

The whole scene was in slow motion. It seemed to go on forever, though it can only have been a couple of moments.

I opened my eyes, and said, 'I don't want to do this any more.' I was so scared.

'What did you see?'

I turned away from the counter, and began tidying a shelf of ceramic angels. At least, I pretended to tidy them. 'I don't want to talk about it.'

'Please,' he touched me on the shoulder. 'Please. What did you see?'

The women had left the shop by now. I think they sensed I needed privacy. I told him. 'This is so weird,' I said. 'I hardly know where to begin.'

'Yes?'

'Do you remember the Dublin bombings? You know. In 1974.'

He nodded. 'Who could forget?'

'I saw that scene again.' He raised his eyebrows, questioningly. 'I was there,' I said. 'I was there that day.'

'What did you see? Just now, I mean. What exactly did you see?'

'I saw a little girl in a pushchair. Just a baby. She was being pushed away from danger. But there wasn't anybody pushing her. It didn't make sense.'

He looked at me, searchingly. 'That,' he said, 'was my daughter.' He explained he was also in town that day. 'I was there with my wife and my child. And just before the bomb went off, you were right, it was as if somebody had pushed my daughter away from danger. Some power. You're right. Something extraordinary did save our child.'

So we had a connection back then, even though we never knew it. That kind of connection happens often in life. So often our paths connect, one way or another.

Simone said, 'This man is meant to come back into your life.'

'But I don't know him. I never knew him before.'

'Even so, you had a connection back then. Your paths crossed. This time you will remain friends. He will help you on a spiritual level.'

I asked the man what his name was, and he said, 'Ah, my name is Vinnie Woods.'

And I said, 'Well, how do you do, Vinnie Woods? My name is Patricia Buckley.' He shook my hand. He had a lovely firm handshake. I liked that. I liked him. I knew I could trust him. 'Do you see angels too?' I asked.

'No.' He shook his head. 'I'm a white witch.'

I burst out laughing. 'You're a what?'

'You see angels – I'm more of a pagan. I work with potions and crystals.'

We got talking then. Vinnie was a very jolly man. He could be a real messer, but he was very strong. He was a very spiritual man too. We became friends from that day. Vinnie told me all about different shows to go to, and how people get together. I liked the sound of that, as there were times I was getting a bit lost because I didn't know if other people did what I did. I'd no idea how many people could see and hear angels and also hear the spirit world. And I was a little bit concerned, even though I had opened up the shop, and had done exactly what the angels had asked me to do.

Vinnie was very good with this. He told me there were lots of different spirit shows all round the country.

'It would be good for you, Trish,' he said. 'Good for you to get a sense of what really goes on.'

'Where are all these shows?'

'Well, as a matter of fact, there is one coming up. It's in the Regency Hotel in Santry.'

'What do you do if you want to go? Do you just buy a ticket?' I really wasn't too sure about this.

'No, no,' he said. 'You just go in. I think it's about five euros on the door. You just go in and you'll see different types of therapists there.'

It was on a Sunday and I decided to go. But when I arrived I could not believe the amount of people in there. There were people selling crystals and stones, but more interesting to me, there were also people doing angel card readings.

There was a lovely energy. That came partly from the music, and partly from the crystals, angels and lotions all set out on the tables. I spotted one table which was absolutely beautiful. The table was covered in a red cloth, with a band of white going through it. And in the centre was this beautiful statue of an angel. There were white feathers sprinkled around and a beautiful purple crystal – an amethyst. There was no reader there, but for some reason I felt drawn to the table.

I remember saying to Simone, 'I've no intention of getting a reading done. So why am I being pulled to this table?'

Andrew said, 'Sure, put your name down.'

'No. I don't think so.'

'Oh, go on. Put it down.'

The lady on the stall said the chap had just gone on a break. She asked did I want a reading.

'Yeah, go on. I wouldn't mind.'

'Come back in about half an hour. He'll be back here by then.' So I pottered around looking at the stalls, but my eyes kept being drawn back to that table. Finally he arrived, and I sat down. There were three decks of cards on the table.

He said, 'Pick a deck.' I picked the middle deck. It said 'Healing with the Angels'. He told me to split the deck in three. I did that and handed them back. He picked out three cards, then looked up, and made eye contact with me. He shook his head slightly. 'I don't know why you're sitting there,' he said.

'Well, to get an angel reading, I hope.'

'You don't need to be sitting here. You could do my reading if you really wanted to.'

'Oh, I don't know,' I said. 'I'm only just back, and I'm not sure if I should be doing this work or not.'

'Well, your guardian angel is telling my guardian angel that yes, you should be back. They are welcoming you back.' He gazed at me a bit more. 'There is this amazing white light all around you. This light could come out of your hands.'

'I do feel a lot of heat coming from my hands sometimes,' I said. 'And I know when people are sick, and I know when they are suffering.'

'And what you feel is real.' I never did get my reading. Not that day. We ended up chatting, and he refunded my money. 'It was a real pleasure to meet you.'

I liked going to the shows, because of the energy with so many practitioners gathered together. I noticed that many of the people who did angel readings had completed some kind of training. That made me wonder if I should train too. At one stage I rang Mary K Hayden, because she runs really good courses in angel therapy. I told her I was thinking of taking one, and she just laughed.

'You don't need to take a course, Patricia! Just carry on doing what you're doing.' Hearing her say that gave me such confidence.

When she told me I didn't need training, Andrew suddenly popped up.

'Told you!' he said. 'Didn't I always say I could teach you more than any course?' And it's true. He had always said that.

'Patricia, if you take training you will go off the road. Your powers won't be as good, because you'll be trained in a different way than you know.' I trusted him, and I still trust him. Because he has never ever seen me wrong.

17 Essie

I can't heal people, but I can be a channel for healing.

One day three sisters came into the shop. They were looking at angels, and particularly at the decks of angel cards. There was something about them that I really liked. I couldn't help but connect with them. We got chatting, and it was almost like I'd known them all my life. It was strange, because I'd never met them before. Their names were Patricia, Tina and Anne.

They'd all come in quite often after that. Anne lived in Belfast, but whenever she was down in Dublin she would come and visit the angel shop. I remember, one day, when we'd been chatting for a long time, she wanted to give me a hug. She did, and I thought that was beautiful.

All the sisters would talk about their mammy.

'I wish you could meet her,' they'd say. 'You'd love her, but she's confined to her bed.' She'd been really ill and she was on oxygen twenty-four hours a day. As the weeks went on, they talked about their mammy more and more. They'd told her all about me and about the shop.

One day, Patricia said, 'My ma would love an angel reading.' I'd never given an angel reading.

But I said, 'Right.' Then I said, 'Oh, sure, I'll do it for her.' I don't know what made me say that. I was surprised after I'd said it. Maybe the angels gave me a good clatter to get the words out.

'There's just one thing,' she said. 'My ma is completely confined to the bed. She can't come out.'

'Oh, sure. I'll go up and see her.'

The joy on Patricia's face when I said that I would go up and visit! 'Would you do that?'

'Sure, I will.'

'Of course we'll pay you.'

I was surprised at that. 'Sure, what would I need money for? Just for going up to see a lady who would like to have a little angel reading done.'

When Patricia left, I was shaking. I wondered how I was going to get out of *that* one. *Perhaps*, I thought, *I can pretend I'm sick*. But I can't lie. I never could. So Stephen drove me to Essie's house. I was so scared still. I was wondering how I thought I could give a reading, when I never had before.

Then someone whispered in my ear, 'Don't be so silly.'

I jumped a mile and saw Andrew, my spirit guide, had come too. He was sitting in the middle of the van, between Stephen and myself.

'I wish you wouldn't do that.'

Stephen looked at me sharply.

'Patricia, are you talking to me, or are you talking to an angel? Because I don't know whether to answer you.'

I explained about Andrew, who was chuckling now.

'You're going to be fine, Patricia,' said Andrew.

'You reckon?'

'I know. And you have to do this. This woman, Essie, needs to hear a message.'

We arrived at Essie's house and I was still terrified. Still wondering what would happen. I imagined going to sit by Essie's bed and saying nothing. Patricia answered the door and let me in.

'Welcome!' she said, then she turned and shouted, 'Tina. Angel Trish is here.'

'That's a lovely name,' I said. 'That was a lovely thing to call me.'

'Well, you are, aren't you? You're an earth angel.'

The sisters led me into the front room, where their mother's bed was. And there was Essie Cash. A beautiful, beautiful lady. She was tiny, and so delicate. She was sitting there with her oxygen, looking so dignified. That was the first thing I noticed. There was such a sense of calm in that room.

The second thing I noticed was all the statues that surrounded her in that room. Most of them, I realized, had been bought by the daughters from our shop. There were so many. I saw Our Lady, the Sacred Heart, and Padre Pio. She said, later, she loved Padre Pio the best.

'Ma, this is Angel Trish,' said Patricia. 'She's come up from the angel shop to see you. Isn't she good to come?' And in my head I was thinking, *What am I going to do?* I really did not know what was going to happen.

Essie held out her arms. She said, 'Welcome, child.'

She called me 'child'. And I actually felt like a child. I thought, *Oh, maybe she's not taking me seriously. Or maybe I'm too serious in my head.*

'Hello, Essie.' I pulled up a chair and sat beside the bed, and the girls left the room. They went to make a cup of tea. Myself and Essie chatted for a few minutes. Then I looked up, and in the spirit world I could see this man.

Andrew, who was beside me, said, 'Well, are you going to talk to him?' I was wondering, *Am I really seeing him?* He said, 'Yes. And the lady is waiting.' I was still really unsure.

Then, before I said a word, the spirit man said, 'Howaya?' I laughed at the accent. I looked up and said, 'Hello.'

'Hello to you. My name is Dennis but they call me Dinnie.'

'Well, howaya, Dinnie?'

I turned to Essie then. 'Essie, is your husband's name Dinnie?'

'It is.'

'Well, he's here.'

'Well, sure I know,' she said. 'He's always here.' She sounded so matter of fact about it. She was sensing him. We had a laugh about that. Her mother was there too, and her father. Both of them were in the spirit world. All the angels were around.

Dinnie spoke first. 'Jesus, I thought she would be gone before me,' he said. 'And I had to go before her!'

I relayed the message and Essie started laughing. I relayed the messages backwards and forwards, and it was lovely. It made Essie so happy, and all the messages were positive.

'I've also got sons in the spirit world,' she said. We talked about them then, and we talked about the angels. And she loved the chat.

I said, 'I'll come back and visit you whenever I can.'

'Will you, child?'

'Yes, I will.'

As I left I felt on top of the world. I knew all the angels were around her. Stephen came and picked me up. As we were heading home he said, 'Well, how was that?'

'I don't think I'll ever forget this day for the rest of my life. It was such a wonderful feeling. And as for Essie, she is such a beautiful lady.'

I started to laugh then. 'She called me "child".'

'She did?'

'She did. And that made me feel really special.'

*

About two weeks went by, then Patricia came up to the shop.

'How is your mam? How is Essie?'

'Not the best, Angel Trish. To be honest, I'm worried about her. I think she has an infection.'

'I'm really sorry to hear that. Your mam is such a special lady. Would you like me to call in?'

'Oh, Trish. I don't like disturbing you.'

'That's no problem. Sure, I'll call in on my way home from work.'

I went in, and sure enough, Essie did have an infection. I could sense at once that she wasn't well in herself. But I knew that it wasn't her time to go. I knew, because the Angel Raphael was there, and he told me that it wasn't her time.

'She does have a nasty infection,' he said, 'but she has another year or so before she will pass away.'

I took her hand, and when I did, something strange happened. There was this heat coming from my left side, across my back, and down my arm to the hand that was holding Essie's. Essie felt it too. She opened her eyes and looked at me.

'Oh my God,' she said. 'That's beautiful.' I asked the Angel Raphael what was happening.

He said, 'The divine is giving her healing.'

'But it's not me.'

'No, Patricia. You are only a channel for the divine.'

'Well, thank God for that.'

I can't heal people, but I can ask for healing. And Raphael said that to me.

He said, 'Always remember, Patricia, that you are not a healer. But you are a channel for healing.'

Over the coming days Essie got stronger. And it got so she didn't want the doctor to visit her any more. She wanted me to visit instead, and I did. I loved going to visit Essie. We had a very strong connection, always. She was funny, though. She was so generous that I soon learned never to admire any of her possessions. If I said, 'I like that angel statuette,' or 'That picture is lovely,' Essie would want to give it to me as a present.

Through my friendship with Essie, I became closer to her three daughters, Patricia, Tina and Anne. We got on so well, all of us, that we started describing ourselves as blood sisters.

Meanwhile, Essie recovered well. She was still confined to bed, still on oxygen all the time, but she was stable again, and happy. About two years passed, when I had a call from Patricia.

'My mam is really not well,' she said.

'OK. I'm on my way down.'

'No, Patricia, stay put a moment. I'm sending my nephew, Jason, to collect you. I hate putting you to trouble. I hate disturbing you.' I said it was fine.

When we arrived, I went into the front room, and Essie just looked at me.

'Howaya feeling?'

'Oh,' she said, 'I hate to be disturbing you.'

'No, Essie. You're grand.' I saw all the angels surrounding her. And there was her husband, Dinnie, from the spirit world.

'Ah, she'll be in my arms by Friday night,' he said.

I went into the kitchen where Patricia was making me a cup of tea. Tina was there too. They were both looking at me.

Patricia said, 'Well?'

'Do you want me to tell you the truth?'

'Well, you've never told us lies before. Everything you've ever told us has always been spot on.'

'OK.' I found this so difficult. 'Your mam will be in your dad's arms by midnight on Friday.' This was Wednesday.

'Right so,' said Patricia. Then she picked up the phone and started ringing all the relatives. That worried me a little. I looked at Dinnie, and said, 'You'd better be right.'

'Oh, I am. It's her time now.'

Andrew, my spirit guide, was there too. And he gave me extra reassurance.

'She will go,' he said. 'She will go to heaven. And she won't struggle.'

'Are you sure?' I'd been worried about that. 'She's on oxygen. I would hate her to have a difficult death.'

'I promise you, Patricia, Essie will not struggle.'

Over the next twenty-four hours Essie's relations began to assemble. Anne from Belfast came. All her grandchildren arrived, and her great-grandchildren.

'Patricia, you will stay, won't you?'

'Ah – you won't need me any more.'

'No, Patricia, please.'

They insisted, and told me that I wasn't intruding – that when I was there Essie felt better. So I stayed for a few hours on the Wednesday. I came back home, and went to work, as usual on Thursday. I knew they needed their time, just as a family. But I went back after work on the Thursday.

The house was crowded with relations, coming and going. A couple of her sons were with her in the front room. They were just sitting there beside the bed. One of them was holding her hand. Then, suddenly, Essie sat up in the bed. I will never ever forget that. She sat up and took her oxygen mask off. Patricia ran in, worried she'd start gasping for breath, but she seemed fine. She had a little colour in her cheeks.

'Ma, are you OK?'

She nodded. 'There's just one thing, though.'

'Yes? Ma, what is it?'

'Please can I have a sandwich?' I could see Patricia standing there with her mouth open.

'I'll get it.' Tina had just arrived in the room. She'd heard, and she rushed off to make one.

'Is there anything else, Ma?' asked Patricia.

'Yes, there is.' She turned to her sons. 'Would one of youse please turn on the TV?'

'The TV?' The two men looked at her as if they'd seen a ghost.

'Yes.' She sighed. 'I don't want to miss *EastEnders*. And youse can move out of the way too.'

I was still sitting on the stairs, but that didn't stop me hearing one of Essie's sons giving out about me.

'I don't know who that bleedin' mad one is from the angel shop. Perhaps she should be locked up. Because one thing is for sure: my ma is going nowhere.'

I began to wonder if he was right, and if I had got it very badly wrong. But Andrew popped up then, making me jump, as he generally did.

'You're not wrong. You know that.'

'I hope not. I mean, you know, they're all here.'

'No. It's fine. She's fine. She hasn't long, but she won't need her oxygen. And you can tell the family that.' I did.

'We've not seen our mam without oxygen. Not for the past twenty years.'

'Well, she isn't going to need it.'

For that evening, while Essie was sitting up there in the

bed, it was as if she were a young woman. And she never put the oxygen on again.

She looked wonderful when I went home that night.

On the Friday I worked in the angel shop as usual. After I closed up, I went back to see Essie. She was lying there, quiet again. But she still didn't need the oxygen.

All the family were there, round her bed, and it was lovely. And because the daughters are so into angels, they played this music by the Irish band Bliss, called 'Come into the Light'. It was beautiful. So peaceful.

I remember her sons were on one side of her bed, and her daughters on the other. I remember seeing all the angels around the bed. I knew it wouldn't be long. Patricia, Tina and Anne were all there, in the room, and Marian, Essie's daughter-in-law. Margaret, a daughter I didn't know so well, was whispering in her ear.

She was saying, 'It's OK to go now. You can follow the light.'

And just at that moment, Essie opened her eyes wide.

'I can't see the light,' she said. That was so typical of Essie. Everyone burst out laughing. I knew she still had a couple of hours to go. I was worried, in case she started to suffer.

'Please,' I said to the angels. 'Please don't make her struggle. She's struggled quite enough over the years. Just let her go. Let her go gently.'

Patricia and Tina were still there in the room, and I knew they weren't supposed to be there when their mother passed over. They were the ones who looked after her all the time, and Essie really didn't want them there. Not when she took her last breath. She knew how upset the two of them would get.

Just then, Tina stepped out of the room. She lived next door, and wanted to check something. At that, Patricia looked at me, and asked, 'Will it be long?'

I shook my head. 'No. Not long now.'

'Right. I'll just go and get Tina.'

Then Archangel Michael appeared, and I knew the time had come. Sure enough, Essie took a last breath, then she slipped away. At that moment, Anne gasped and grabbed my hand and held it tight. She held her breath. I knew she'd seen something. I knew, because I could see it too. The spirit of Dinnie, her dad, had come and he had Essie in his arms. Anne's grasp tightened.

'It's OK,' I said. 'You can let go of me now.' Anne still held her breath. 'He's not going to drop her.'

Then she said, 'Did you see that? Are you really seeing that?'

I nodded. I was pleased for her. She'd actually seen heaven. Just for that split second. It had been beautiful for her to see, because she hadn't been there when her dad passed over.

Essie did die before midnight on the Friday. She died at around eleven o'clock, on the same night as Pope John Paul died. It was so amazing, the calmness in that room. It was full of angels. It was just so calm for those three days that she was on her journey into heaven.

That's not the end of the story. Not quite. Because I continued to see Essie. I saw her in the spirit world, and I continue to see her there. Essie always loved her chats. And if she wants me to tell her daughters something, she'll pop in and ask me to pass on a message. It can happen any time. I might be serving in the shop – or getting my breakfast in the morning. I don't mind. I'll always have time for Essie.

18 Dedicating Myself to the Angels

*I put trust in my angels. That trust enables them to
let me see the truth and only the truth.*

We continued working both shops – the grocery shop and
the angel shop. More and more people were coming to visit
the little angel shop at the bottom of the hill. They were
coming from all over, and I met some amazing people.
They'd often stay and chat, telling me their stories, both the
happy ones and the sad.

I never wanted to leave the angel shop. I wanted to be
there more and more. I was meeting so many people, day in
and day out. I was giving out a few messages to people in the
shop, just casually, as they were going in and out. And then I
started to do readings. I really enjoyed it. I was only doing
one or two, but I found myself getting stronger and stronger.
I was listening to Andrew.

He was saying, 'Just go with it.'

'But what if there is nobody there on the other side?'

'Well, then, you just have to be honest.' So that's what I did.

It didn't work with everybody, but for most of the people
who came in I was able to give them a message. I got stronger
and stronger each day with this. Every time I gave someone
a message Andrew and Simone would say, 'Well done. You've
just made that person very happy.' And that's what it's all
about. It's allowing people to know that there is life on the

other side. That just because we leave this life, it doesn't really mean that we die. Because nothing ever dies, and we don't die. Our soul and our spirit live on.

I gave many people proof about that, and it made me really happy. Then we got a chance to move to a bigger angel shop. It was in a lovely location, up the hill in the main part of the village. That was a battle in itself, but we eventually got it and moved into the new Angels of Ireland shop on Main Street in Finglas. That's where we are now. We've been there for six years.

By now we'd given up the grocery shop. The angels asked us to do that. They said we'd have our work cut out running the angel shop, so that's exactly what we did.

I started doing readings, and one day I was asked to go to Belfast to give a day of readings. My first thought was, *Flipping hell, how do I this?* It was for Essie's daughter, Anne. She said I could stay over in her house. We are basically now sisters, so even though I felt uneasy, off I went on the train with Patricia.

I was a bit nervous. I felt I was coming out of my comfort zone but I went. I was going to do five readings one day and five the next. That was a lot of readings for me, and I was really worried. It might sound silly, but the thing that worried me most was the Belfast accent. I thought, *How will I understand it? How will I understand what the spirits are saying?*

We arrived at Anne's on Friday, the day before the first reading. We had dinner with her and went to bed early. I got up early on Saturday. I always wake early on the day of readings. I knew I needed to make sure I was grounded properly and that I had all the angels around me. Anne was brilliant. Her sitting room is like an angel room – a bit like at her mother Essie's house. There were so many angels in there, it was a pleasure to work in. And she lit all the candles for me.

I explained that this could go one way or another.

'I'm worried that the people I'm reading for are your friends, Anne. They might think you gave me information on all of them.'

'But, Patricia, I don't even know who's coming for the readings. I don't know them.'

'Oh, right. So how did you organize it?'

'I just mentioned you and your readings to a few people, and they asked me to tell them if you were coming to Belfast any time.'

As I was sitting in that room waiting for the first person, there was a beautiful young fifteen-year-old spirit girl. She kept saying, 'My mammy. My mammy.'

'OK?'

'My mammy will be here.'

'How did you pass?'

'I did a very silly thing. I took my own life, and for that I'm eternally sorry.'

'For what?'

'For the pain. For the pain my mammy and my daddy went through.'

In came this lovely wee woman. I said my name was Patricia.

'Have you ever had any readings done before?'

'Yes, I have. I've had a few readings done.'

'OK.' I explained the way I work. I explained that if the spirit world doesn't come through, it doesn't mean anything is wrong. I don't call the spirit world. I wait for them to contact me. She was beautiful, this lady.

'OK.'

I suppose living in Belfast they had a lot of troubles. I believe they are very strong people because of everything that has gone on there. I could feel the love that this woman had for everybody, it didn't matter what religion. I took both her hands. And as I took her hands the young girl appeared to me again.

'Hello, Mammy.'

The woman started to cry. I allowed her tears to flow for a while because it was healing for her. The girl gave me all the messages for her mother, and the woman ended up with me in the room for nearly an hour. It was the most wonderful experience to give her proof that heaven really does exist and that when we die we do go to heaven. We don't really die because our souls and our spirits live on. Our body is a shell and it is what is inside us that lives on.

'Thank you,' she said, when I'd finished handing on the messages. 'I feel on top of the world. It is wonderful to know that my wee girl is safe and is happy.'

I held her hands and smiled at her.

'Most of all, though, I'm happy to know that it wasn't my fault. That it wasn't anything I did or said that made her take her life.'

The next reading was lovely too. The girl came in, and behind her I could see a really dark man. He looked Indian, but she wasn't dark.

'This man is telling me that he's your father. He says that you've been looking for him.'

'Yes, that's true.'

'Well, obviously you know now that he is on the other side. But you are going to find relatives: aunts and uncles and maybe some cousins.'

'I've been trying for a couple of years. I mean, I've been trying to reach my father. I've been to readings before, but he never came through.'

I explained that he was there. He explained why he hadn't

been there for her as a child. He said it was because he met her mother in London. And she then left him to return to Belfast. When I finished the reading, the girl gave me the biggest hug ever.

There were lots of good readings for those two days in Belfast, and when they had finished, I felt so happy.

I said it to Andrew, 'I feel so privileged that I can pass a message on from heaven.'

And I do. Every day I thank Andrew and Simone, and Archangel Michael who is the most wonderful, wonderful angel. I constantly thank him because he has helped me throughout my life.

My journey has been wonderful. When I look back I see that things happened that were beyond the angels' control. They can't control people's actions. They can't control what other people do, but what they can do is help us if we allow them to do so. And it is so important to ask your angels for help. They are always standing by. They are waiting for us to ask. Please trust: sometimes you may not get that message straight away, but it will come.

I tell people this after I've done a reading. I've been asked back to Belfast quite a lot, but I haven't gone too often. Mostly, I do readings at home.

If you ask me for an angel reading, I'll take you into the room above the Angels of Ireland shop. It's a peaceful room with some angel statues. I light some candles, and maybe play some gentle music. Then I ask you if you've ever had a reading before. It doesn't matter if you believe in angels or not. It doesn't make a difference. They walk with us anyway.

I let the spirit world know I am here. I make sure I ask for blessings, so Andrew, my spirit guide, knows I am ready. He knows who is in the spirit world, and who is meant to come in. Usually, someone from the spirit world will come forth.

Andrew opens the doorway to the spirit world for me, and he brings the spirit person in. They will tell me what is going on in your life, and what questions you need answering. Your guardian angel will be there too. They give me guidance. I pass on any messages, and when all the messages have been passed on, Andrew gently closes the channel between heaven and earth. That's the way I work.

And if there's nothing there at all, I will say so. The angels never allow me to lie. But sometimes they won't give me the information. They won't put me through to the spirit so I can't pass on any messages. It doesn't mean anything is wrong. It just means the spirit world is not ready. I don't force it. That is the one thing the angels don't want me to do. I could do that if I wanted to. But then you don't know what you are getting into, and it could be very dangerous, so I don't do that.

People relax when they come for an angel reading. If they come in with a headache, they feel that headache lift. And when they leave they are full of energy. They tell me that after a reading they sleep very well. This is because I always ask the angels to give them healing for whatever part of their life needs that healing, and I ask the angels to give them that positive energy.

I never did train to give angel readings. Andrew was right, I didn't need to. Everything I know, I learned from the angels. If someone comes for a reading I might not get anything from the spirit world at all. That doesn't mean something bad has happened; it just means they're not supposed to hear anything at that time. That doesn't happen often. It's only ever happened to me about three times.

The times it did happen, I had to be honest. I remember clearly the third time it happened. A girl came to me, and there was nothing there. I said, 'There are no spirits here. I have no messages for you. We'll try again another day.'

And she said, 'Well, could you just read the angel cards for me please? I've heard you're really brilliant.'

'I'm sorry, but I can't do that. I don't do the cards until the end of a reading. If I try, the card reading will be false.'

The girl was disappointed, but she accepted that. And she *did* come back to me a little bit later. That time there was a spirit there, and the reading was fine.

Some readings last for an hour. Some go on longer, and others might only be fifteen minutes long. It just depends what the spirit world wants to say. I don't add anything on. I only see four people in one day, and I don't do readings every day. I can't. I get tired, and I don't want to disrespect the spirit world. If I get tired, I won't be able to hear the spirits clearly.

Sometimes people from the spirit world can be very persistent, especially when they really need to get a message to someone. It can be any time. But Andrew tries to look after me. He warns me that there can be messers. He puts his hand out, and says, 'No,' or he'll say, 'Don't do it.'

Sometimes I ignore him. I say, 'It'll be fine.'

Then it will all get too much. Sometimes I get so tired, and then end up with a kidney infection or something. When that happens he'll say, 'I warned you!'

Nine times out of ten the spirits I see look as old as they were when they passed over, but sometimes they come back to me as a younger person. It's up to them. Spirits always have this nice healthy glow around them. They'll say, 'I don't have the pain any more,' or 'I don't suffer from any ailment.'

Spirits can be messers. And they can be quite funny as well. I was doing a reading once, and the spirit man was playing the spoons. I couldn't believe the noise of it. I had to say to him, 'I can't hear you because of the spoons.'

It was his daughter who was in with me. When I told her she just burst out laughing. She said, 'Oh, that is my dad for you.'

He continued playing the spoons for a little while. It meant that the girl could feel her dad in the room, and it was really lovely for her.

The angels don't give bad news. It is always positive, but they do warn of things that could go wrong. One time I was giving a reading to a chap, and there was something wrong with his motorbike. His guardian angel told me to tell him. I did, but he said, 'No. There's nothing wrong with it.'

'I'm telling you, there is.'

'Oh, fair play,' he said. 'I'll double-check it, but I *know* there's nothing wrong with it.' He left, but came back into the shop five minutes later.

'I apologize,' he said. 'You were right. There's a problem with the back brake. If I'd driven off, the back wheel could have locked.'

Another girl came in for a reading. She said, 'I'm only here because my friend told me to come. She told me that you're very good.'

'OK.'

She looked embarrassed. 'But I'm not really a believer.'

'That's fine,' I said. 'That doesn't matter.' Nobody from the spirit world came to her, but her guardian angel was there. She told me this girl was pregnant. I don't normally read for anyone who is pregnant. Unborn babies can be very sensitive to the change in energy. They sense the spirits and that can upset them. Also, you can get a false reading.

'Are you pregnant?' I asked.

She looked at me. She seemed shocked. 'No! No, I'm not.'

'But you are.'

'I'm not.' She was fiddling with her nails. 'I thought I was, but I've done a test. It's negative.'

I asked her guardian angel was she sure. 'Yes. She is pregnant, and she should go and get another test. She has been worrying about the pregnancy. She doesn't know how to tell her family.'

I went ahead with the reading. She insisted. Her guardian angel told me she was thinking about leaving her job. 'Tell her not to leave. With her being pregnant, changing jobs would be the wrong decision.'

About a week later the girl came into the shop with a bunch of flowers for me.

'You were right,' she said. 'I am pregnant, but last week I was literally just two weeks gone. I was going to leave my job and go travelling. Thanks to you I didn't do that.' She was really pleased she knew.

I love talking to spirits. I could talk to them all day. I can talk to them anywhere. I don't have to be in my special room. That's my problem, you see. Sometimes I forget that talking to spirits can make me tired.

The other day a young couple came into the shop. They only came in to buy some rose quartz crystals, but I happened to look at the young lady, and her dad in the spirit world was standing behind her. He said to me, 'Please tell my daughter I am OK. She's going back to Australia tomorrow.'

I said I would.

'My daughter is really worried,' he said. 'She's having to sell a house back in Australia, and she thinks it will upset me. Please tell her that it's OK. It's OK with me.'

I passed the message on to the girl. She looked at me, and she burst into tears.

'Are you OK?' Her boyfriend put his arm around her.

'I'm fine. I'm just so relieved. I was so worried about it – and about my father. It's a relief to hear he's fine. And he's saying it's OK about the house.'

Once, a woman came to me who I could not help. She was a Filipino, and her husband was Irish. They came into the shop as I was closing up, and he asked me would I give her a reading. This was just before Halloween. I don't normally give readings around then, but this time I said I would.

Stephen had gone out. A big delivery had just arrived, and he was loading it into the van. I took the woman to the back of the shop, but when I looked at her, I noticed her eyes were going white.

Then Archangel Michael stood in front of me and said, 'Don't look at her.'

As he said that, Stephen walked in the door, and he noticed the chair I was sitting in being lifted by some power. The woman spat at me. She was possessed, and her husband started making the sign of the cross. Archangel Michael told me to stand my ground, he kept saying that, 'Stand your ground!' I stood up and said the guardian angel prayer.

She kept trying to get at me. It was like a battle between good and bad spirits. I had a set of rosary beads in my hand, which she did not like. She was actually hissing. Her husband told me afterwards that he had brought her to many priests and they had run away from her. I managed to stand my ground. I was calm. I asked her to leave, but she had sapped my energy. I was completely exhausted for a week after she had been in the shop.

19 Searching for the Missing

I can't force a spirit to come. But if they wish to
communicate with me they can.

Around 2004, I started having these dreams. This was going
on for a lot of nights, and I started feeling really tired. I didn't
know what to do. Then one night, at about three in the morning, I felt a tap, tap on my shoulder. I remember sitting up in
the bed, and there was a young spirit lady. She was very pretty
with blonde hair. I could see that she was pregnant.

She said, 'Please help me.'

I didn't know what to do.

'I'm sorry. But I don't know how to help you.'

She looked at me helplessly, and then she went away. She
came again another night. And she kept coming to me, more
and more. This was going on for quite a while, and I wasn't
getting much sleep. I started getting up and writing down
what she was saying to me. To me it was all a muddle, and I
got really upset when she came. Then I started getting bad
pains. It was as if I was taking on her pain.

While I was writing things down, she would say, 'Castle.'
But I didn't know what she meant. Then she'd say, 'Fiona.'

'Is that your name?'

'Yes, my name is Fiona.' It took me an awful long time to
understand what she meant. It took weeks and weeks and
weeks and I had so much written down. It turned out her

name was Fiona Pender, and she had gone missing when she was seven and a half months pregnant. She was terribly upset. I found it so hard, because I didn't know what to do with this information.

I rang Vinnie Woods and I told him what had happened.

He said, 'OK. Calm down, Patricia. She's communicating with you because she needs your help.'

'But, Vinnie, I don't know what to do. I really don't.' The strangest thing had happened, because I thought I was going completely mad here. I didn't know this spirit girl. I didn't know her family. Why was she coming to me?

Then something even stranger happened. I was contacted by this man called Eddie (not his real name). To this day I really don't know how that happened. Eddie was on a trace team who worked on all the missing girls in Ireland.

Eddie had heard of me. I don't know how, but he knew I was a psychic medium. He heard that I was very good at what I did. That's why he made contact with me. When Eddie made contact with me, my nerves were shattered. I thought, *Oh my God. What if I'm wrong?*

Andrew, my spirit guide, got cross with me then.

He said, 'Patricia, you really are going to have to stop asking yourself if you are wrong.'

Eddie asked for a meeting. He said he'd call in the evening. I rang Vinnie again, and told him what had happened.

I said, 'Would you please be here with me when Eddie calls?' He agreed.

Vinnie came up and after we had had a cup of tea I took him into the angel room I have in my house and I lit my candles like I always do. I asked Archangel Michael could he please help me to explain properly about this spirit girl who kept coming through to me.

It really helped me that Vinnie was there.

He said, 'Close your eyes. Hold my hand, and just relax.' Which I did. I completely relaxed and as I closed my eyes, Andrew was there with me. Now Andrew can be a bit of a messer at times. He is the type of spirit guide who cheers me up, and makes me feel comfortable and competent. But he can also be very serious when he needs to be.

He was standing there and he was saying, 'You are going to be fine. Everything is going to be fine. When you open your eyes the doorway to heaven is going to open.' I loved that, because I had seen the doorway to heaven many, many times before and it is the most beautiful thing to see. It's just like this little archway, and there's this massive white light coming through it. The light was so bright, you would think you would need your strongest pair of sunglasses for it, but it does not hurt your eyes. It is just beautiful. When that door opens, the most wonderful feeling of calm, peace and serenity comes through from heaven.

Andrew wasn't the only angel there. My guardian angel Simone was there too, and the Archangel Michael. He had his sword. He wanted to make sure that nothing negative was going to come in.

I said to Vinnie, 'Oh God, I hope I'm right on this.'

And Vinnie started laughing. He said, 'Do you know what, you're only gas! One day you're going to pat yourself on the back and say, "Well done."'

That would be hard for me to do because the angels always taught me to be grounded and never to think I was better than anyone else. To me we are all equal in God's eyes.

I got myself very relaxed, and then I heard the doorbell go. Stephen was in that night, so he let Eddie in. Hearing his voice, I came back to normality, and said, 'Oh God, what will I do?'

'You'll be fine,' said Vinnie. 'You'll be fine.'

We walked into the sitting room, and I saw that Eddie wasn't alone. He had another detective with him. And there they were, all official with their notebooks. I gave them a cup of tea and then they said what they'd heard about me. Eddie is a great believer in the psychic world. That was a great help. It made me feel relaxed. They came into the angel room. Vinnie stayed in the sitting room, so I turned to him.

'Vinnie, do me a favour. Sit in with me on this one.'

He smiled, and stood up. 'Of course. But only if I'm allowed.'

'Of course you're allowed.' I laughed. ' I'm not being questioned for a crime.'

So in he came. There was myself, Vinnie, Eddie and the other detective. We were sitting there and they started asking me questions.

'All I know is this young spirit lady keeps giving me messages. And I don't know what to do with the messages.'

I was waiting for Fiona to start giving me messages and she didn't. I remember sitting there saying, 'Oh my God, what am I going to do?'

I looked at Vinnie. We connect very well. He is a powerful man, but when we're connecting spiritually we're really strong together. It's like my spirit energy knows what Vinnie's spirit energy is doing and Vinnie is very dedicated and committed to what he does as a white witch.

I couldn't answer any of the questions Eddie was asking me. Then all of a sudden I looked, and behind Eddie I saw the archway to heaven, and the light behind him. And the doorway opened up. Coming through the doorway were two men.

'Eddie, your brother and your father are here from the spirit world.'

He looked at me and said, 'What?'

'They both have the same name,' I said, and he nodded. And then his father and brother told me what had happened to them. Then they gave me some personal messages for Eddie from heaven.

I was confused. I said to Andrew, 'Why are you after doing that? He came up here to ask about Fiona Pender. And Fiona doesn't come through and it ends up that Eddie receives a message from heaven.'

'That was the way it was meant to be,' said Andrew. 'Just for now, Patricia. Because Eddie is a believer, but the detective with him is not. And they have to convince their head office that what you do is real.'

'OK, then.' So I passed the messages on. After half an hour Eddie thanked me and went out of the room. Vinnie went out after him. I could hear the kettle going and they were having a cup of tea. That left me with the other detective, who said to me, 'How long have you been doing this work?' I explained what had happened to me when I was younger. I told the detective I wasn't long back at it, but the spirit world was coming back to me at a fast pace.

'I can't force them to come. But if they wish to communicate with me they can.'

I was picking some books off the floor, and as I turned around Fiona came through from the spirit world.

'This detective was there on the search in my flat when I went missing,' she said.

'Really?'

'Yes.'

I said that to the detective, who went a bit white.

'Yes, I was there, but that was never public knowledge.'

'No, Fiona is just telling me.' It ended up that I gave the

detective a personal message too. We have since become friends and the detective contacts me whenever he's in need of my help on a psychic level.

I was completely exhausted by the end of that evening. After that night, Fiona started coming through more and more. She told me the name of a road in Tullamore. Then she told me the name of a butcher's shop. Then she talked about bus stops. I thought, *What am I going to do with all this information?* I'd never been to Tullamore in my life, but I jotted it all down.

I said to Stephen, 'What will I do with this? What is she trying to tell me?'

'Why don't we go and find out?'

So we got into the car and we drove to Tullamore. I realized when I got there what she meant. All these places existed. We went to Charleville Castle. I thought maybe Fiona had been saying that was where she was buried. It was quite spooky – there are spirits running around there, but it's a beautiful place too. I think now that Fiona was saying, 'I'm real. What I'm telling you is real. Please listen to me.' I did do that.

After a couple of weeks she finally brought me to her mother's door. I will never ever forget that day for as long as I live.

There was I walking up the drive to Fiona Pender's mother's house. I thought, *Oh God. Please help me with this.* Andrew said, 'It will be fine.'

I was shaking. Stephen stayed in the car. I thought, *What do I do? What do I say?* But I knew I had to do this. Fiona was so strong with me. She wanted her mother to know she was safe in heaven. And even though she was still missing, she *was* safe in heaven. She wasn't lost, and she wasn't upset.

I shook from head to toe. My heart was pounding as I knocked on that door. A young man answered the door. He was a lovely-looking guy, who could only have been in his early twenties. He opened the door and he looked at me.

'I'm not some madwoman,' I said. 'But tell me, is this Fiona Pender's mother's house?'

'Are you a reporter?'

'God, no. I am not a reporter. I promise you that. I am a psychic medium. Fiona has been communicating with me and she's led me here to this house.'

He looked at me again.

'Just hold on one minute.' He left the door slightly open, and I waited. I expect only two or three minutes had passed, but to me it felt like a lifetime. Looking down the driveway I could see Stephen in the car, and I felt like running to him. I said, 'Oh, Andrew, what is happening?'

I could imagine the police coming to take away the madwoman who was knocking at this woman's door. That didn't happen. What did happen was almost as bad. After a few minutes, the door closed. I stood staring at the closed door. Nobody came to it. Nobody answered. Nothing.

'Andrew, now what do I do?'

'You get back in the car. You go home. You've made the first contact, now you must wait.'

I knew he was right but it was hard, walking away from that door. Myself and Stephen were both quiet on the journey home. I was feeling low, and Stephen could see that. I didn't know what to make of it all. But at the same time, I knew I had to trust Andrew, and to trust what the angels were giving me. I knew I just had to go with it, and that's exactly what I did.

*

Fiona never stopped communicating with me. At the time I was developing my readings and gaining in confidence. Fiona was there all the time. Every night she would tap me on the shoulder. It got to the stage that it was just little chats she wanted. I never lost the feeling that I would, one day, meet up with her mother. So I began to write down all the things she was telling me. Even the things that didn't seem anything to do with her disappearance.

There would be nights when I was so tired, and then I would say, 'Would you ever leave me alone and let me sleep?' She was a real little night owl. She liked it that I could see her and hear her, and she told me that one day I would meet her mother.

One Friday evening, myself and Stephen were in the sitting room, tired after work, just yakking. We had the TV on, but we had the volume turned low. We weren't taking any notice of the TV, we were just talking over the events of the week.

'Fiona is here for some reason,' I said, and as I said it we both turned and looked at the TV. There was Josephine Pender on *The Late Late Show* talking about Fiona. We turned the television up and I decided I'd ring *The Late Late Show*. I left a message and my phone number with them. I explained that I had been receiving messages, and I asked could they pass my number on.

About two weeks went by. Then a man rang, saying he was acting for Josephine Pender. He asked if she could please meet up with me.

'Of course she can.'

'She has said she will travel to you.'

I didn't think that would be right. Fiona had told me that her mother suffered from ill health. So I said, 'No, that's OK.

I can travel to meet her.' I asked if she could drop something of Fiona's with me. Maybe a piece of jewellery. So Stephen and I went back to Tullamore and booked into a hotel for that night. We were having dinner in the hotel, when I got a message to say that there was a young man in reception looking for me. I went out. It was the young man who had opened the door to me all those weeks ago.

He said, 'I'm really sorry for disturbing you.'

'You're not. It's fine.'

'But you're having your dinner.'

'Really, it's OK. Would you like to sit down?'

He shook his head. 'It's just that my mother asked me to bring these few bits up to you. They belonged to my sister Fiona.' He said his name was John. He sat and talked to me for a while. He didn't say anything about the time he'd shut the door on me. I didn't either. I understood the family's hurt and pain. But he looked a bit embarrassed.

'Thank you for bringing these up, John. I promise you, I'll take good care of them. And when I meet your mother I will bring it all back.'

He thanked me. Then he said, 'Can we please pay you?'

I shook my head. 'No. I don't want you to pay me anything. I'm not here to get money. I'm here because your sister wants me to be here.'

I brought the bag up to the room. I knew I needed to rest well that night. I asked Andrew to make sure no spirits came through. He could be good like that. I slept well and got up really early the next morning. We had breakfast, then Stephen went off for a walk. I needed to meditate because I needed a quiet mind. I had to make sure what I was sensing or feeling was 100 per cent for Josephine Pender.

I opened the bag and found a red jacket. There were also

two rings. One was an engagement ring, the other a wedding ring. There was also a photo of Fiona. She was a beautiful-looking girl, exactly as I would see her, with her long blonde hair. I laid all the items out on the bed, and I picked up the jacket.

I heard Fiona then. She said, 'I loved that jacket.'

I closed my eyes, and again she showed me the castle she had mentioned so many times before.

'That's Charleville Castle. I used to model wedding dresses there. I modelled there many times.'

I put the engagement ring on my finger and this voice said, 'That's my ring.'

But this time it wasn't Fiona. It was her grandmother's spirit who had come through. 'I passed that down to Josephine.' I wrote that down.

Nobody came to claim that wedding ring. It was Fiona's, but she wasn't married and she didn't want me to wear it. I respected that and I took the ring off.

I had arranged to meet Josephine at her house at one o'clock. It felt strange going back to that house. I remembered the last time, when I had to retreat back down the drive. I remembered how helpless and low that had made me feel. I was nervous today, but at least I felt sure of a welcome.

The first thing that struck me about Josephine was how tiny she was. The second thing that struck me was her warmth. The minute I walked in that door, she enveloped me in the warmest, warmest hug. That warmth was genuine. There was another girl there. She was a friend of Fiona's.

They were being very cautious with me. That was perfectly fine. I could understand that. Fiona had been missing for so many years – she went missing from her flat in August 1996 – and they had spoken to so many people about her disappearance. Josephine explained about the closed door. She said they'd had reporters up there just the day before my first visit and the reporters had given them a hard time.

I sat with Josephine. I handed back Fiona's belongings.

'The engagement ring.'

'Yes?'

'I understand that wasn't actually Fiona's? That it belonged originally to her grandmother, and was passed on to you, Josephine?'

Josephine cried. 'You're right. The ring was my mother's.'

'And the jacket,' I said. 'Fiona loved that jacket.'

'You're right. She did love it.'

'Your son Mark is in the spirit world too.' He had been killed in a motorcycle crash a year or so before Fiona went missing.

'You're right.'

'Well, they're all together.'

'What about Sean? What about my husband, Fiona's father?'

He, I knew, had been devastated over Fiona's disappearance. Especially when it came after Mark's death. The couple had searched and searched, and when there had been no sign of Fiona, he just couldn't take it any more. So from a happy family of five – soon to be a family of six – just two were left. Just Josephine and her son John. How Josephine coped with such loss, I do not know. First she lost her son in an accident. Then her only daughter, who was seven and a half months pregnant, disappeared, never to be seen again. Then she lost her husband too. She is the strongest woman I've met in my entire life. She's had to be. I admire her so much. I admire her faith and her strength. She is never going to give up until Fiona is found.

Josephine asked me if I would mind going on a drive.

'Stephen, would you mind driving, but taking my directions?'

'Of course I will.'

Stephen was driving, John was in the front seat, and myself and Josephine were in the back of the car. John was giving directions to Stephen along the country roads. I had some rosary beads in my pocket. I took them out and began to say the rosary. I'm not overly religious. I never was, but I've always had a devotion to Our Lady, and to St Bernadette. I closed my eyes and held my rosary beads. I was in a world of my own. I couldn't see where we were going, because I was concentrating on listening to Fiona. It was quite a bumpy road.

All of a sudden I shouted the words, 'Stop the car.'

'Oh Jesus!' Josephine had grabbed my arm.

I began to cry. I felt full of energy, and I needed to get out of the car. I really needed to.

Stephen said, 'But there's nothing here. There's nothing.'

'But I have to get out.' I climbed out of the car, and Josephine got out too.

'My God.'

'She's here. I can feel she's here.'

Fiona kept saying to me, 'Here I am.'

I was looking around and it was just field after field. I climbed over a fence, and I could hear her, 'Here I am. Here I am.'

'Fiona darling, I can hear you. I just can't see you.' And there were feathers. White feathers flying everywhere. Feathers are a symbol from the spirit world that you are on the right track, or you are in the right place. And it hurt me because I knew she was there but I couldn't find her.

I searched those fields for hours and hours, but all I could say was, 'Please find peace in heaven. Because one day, one day, your killer will be brought to court. And you will be found. And you will be buried with your brother and your father.'

After walking round that field for so long, I was totally exhausted.

For legal reasons we cannot name that place where I, Josephine Pender and a lot of other people believe Fiona is. Fiona told me who her killer was. But there is no proof, so the police cannot act. But I do believe one day Fiona will be found and will be laid to rest with her baby. Meanwhile, I know that she is happy in heaven. And she's not struggling.

Josephine and I have become friends since that day and we keep in constant contact with each other. She thanked me for the comforting messages I gave her from Fiona. I will never give up the search for Fiona. I don't go searching those fields any more, because I know that one day, all of those missing girls will be found. They will.

Around that time I was getting messages from another missing person. She wasn't as strong as Fiona, but she did get me to speak to her mother on the phone. She was very persistent. She kept saying to me that her mam was at her uncle's. I did manage to get a contact number and I passed on a message to the mother. Then the girl asked me to go out into the countryside. I did that. I'm not a walker, I don't keep fit, but when I got to the place she told me, I began to walk very fast. I can't normally do that. Yet I didn't get out of breath and I wasn't tired. When I got back I rang the young woman's mother. She burst out laughing.

'My daughter was a professional walker,' she said. 'She just loved to walk. That is why you felt the way you did. She was letting you know she was with you.'

Spirits do play games with you; they're not dreary. And that was this girl's game with me. Maybe she brought me to the mountains as an indication that she is buried there. I'm sure she is there somewhere. I know people will ask why I can't say exactly where the missing girls are buried, but it's not that easy.

I wish it was as simple as naming a place, but you are looking through their eyes, and they were, maybe, put in a boot of a car. They may not have known where they were going. They give you little hints, like maybe a road sign, and I write that down and find out where it is. It is like this massive jigsaw puzzle. It can take a long time and it is difficult, because it hurts me. It hurts me that they are lost.

All I can say to the families is, I know they will be found. I know the angels want them to be found. It has been many years since they went missing, but they will be found. I pray for them every single night. I light a candle and ask for a guiding light to help whoever it is who will find them. It's hard to get the authorities to search, but I do believe that there are two other girls with this girl, and justice will be done.

Angels have always said, 'Just pass your messages on, that's all you can do.' I pray every night that the day will come when those families can lay their loved ones to rest.

A couple came into the shop back in 2006. The man's brother-in-law had disappeared. He suffered with depression and had been missing for a few days without his medication. I thought to myself, *Please, God, not another one gone missing.* They asked could they speak with me. I agreed and took them into the room upstairs. Andrew told me that the man had not passed over, but that he was seriously ill.

The family had been searching for him high and low. They

were frantic, especially as it was very cold. It was freezing. The angels told me to tell the couple that the young man wasn't dead. He was still alive but only just.

'They tell me you have already searched near where your brother-in-law is.'

'That isn't possible. We searched so thoroughly.'

'Well, you need to go back again. You'll get a feeling in your tummy when you near the place. When you feel that, you must turn back and walk up the street. It's near a place where there is a bus terminus, a laneway and a pub.'

The next day the man arrived in the shop with a big bunch of flowers.

'These are for you.'

'Why?'

'We've found him.'

'You have?'

'You were right. We couldn't find him there. We'd given up, truth be told, and we were about to walk away. But my wife remembered your words. You said, "Turn back and walk up the street." My brother-in-law was lying in a doorway freezing cold. He said he'd been moving about a lot. By the time we found him he was very ill. He really needed his medication. He had to go into hospital because of his depression. But thanks to you we found him. That is what matters.'

I only wish that all my stories could have a happy ending, but they don't, and I suppose we just have to accept it – but that was one happy ending.

20 Travels with the Angels

Our Lady is here. And she will be giving healing to
whoever needs that healing.

In 2005 one of my dreams came true. At last, after years of
wanting to go to Lourdes – of thinking about it, and dreaming about it – at last I got there. And it was the most amazing
experience I've had in my life.

When I stepped off the plane, I didn't know what to expect.
We had to get a coach to our hotel. There are hundreds and
hundreds of shops in Lourdes. I thought, *Where is the grotto?*
Someone who had been there many times directed me there.
When I walked through those gates, I felt this amazing sense
of peace. As I sat there in the grotto, lit with its hundreds
of candles, I felt, even more deeply, a connection with Our
Blessed Lady. I've always had a connection with her, ever since
I was a little girl. I see her as a mother who is trying to protect
her children.

I have never seen Our Lady. That doesn't matter, because
when I felt her presence, I knew her, and I felt she was with
me, and always had been with me. I felt I had been to the
grotto at Lourdes before, although, of course, I had never
been. I felt that this was where I was meant to be. I felt I was
at home.

That is a feeling that has stayed with me, and will, I know, stay with me for the rest of my life. Every year since, I made it my business to go back to Lourdes. It wasn't that I needed healing for myself. It was the sense of peace.

There were thousands of people there in the grotto. When I looked around I could see all their guardian angels. And I saw a mist at the grotto area. I asked a few people if they could see the mist, and they couldn't. But every time I went there I could see it. It was very calm there and this little breeze would come out of nowhere.

I'd always say, 'Our Lady is here. And she will be giving healing to whoever needs that healing.'

I would pray for people who were ill. I also pray when I'm there for those who are missing. It is an amazing experience.

I'm a great believer in Our Lady. Last year, after Lourdes, Stephen and I joined a pilgrimage to Fatima. I'd never been there before. I'd heard that if you go three times round the Basilica, on your knees, and say the rosary as you go, Our Lady grants you a favour.

I wanted to ask Our Lady a favour, and I thought, *I can do that!* So I began. I began one day at seven in the morning, with Maura, Anne and Agnes, three other women from our pilgrimage, but it wasn't easy. It wasn't raining, but it had rained on the two days before, so the ground was wet.

I didn't realize how far it was. It was difficult. I have a bad hip, and my back started hurting. I was wondering if I would ever make it. Then I got a stone stuck in my knee. It really hurt.

'How will I do this?'

Stephen was standing beside me. He put his hand out and said, 'Trish, you don't have to do this.'

'I'm not stopping now. But I really need some help.'

Then I spoke to my brother John, who is now in the spirit world. I said, 'John, I need some strength here. I don't care if you kick me in the backside. I need to do this.'

As I said those words, this dog came from nowhere, through the Basilica. It lay on the ground beside me. I said, 'Oh, dog, if you want to help me, you're going to have to move.'

That dog walked beside me, and helped me, and as soon as I got to the Basilica, it looked at me, saw I looked stronger, and walked off. My brother had rescued dogs from everywhere. The only sign I could get from John would be a dog or a guitar. I knew it was John who had helped me.

I managed to complete the three circles round the Basilica that day. And this year, 2010, Our Lady granted the favour which I had asked for Kym and her husband, Larry. I asked her to grant them the gift of a baby, and Kym has now been doubly blessed with twins.

Freya and Sean were born twelve weeks premature and weighed a mere 890 and 900 grams respectively. Three weeks after they were born little Sean had a small setback and a bit of a scare, so Kym decided to ask God and the angels to give her a sign and, if possible, to make the sign something to do with the number two, so that she would know both her babies would be OK. Kym went to the hospital the next evening and on entering the ICU she spotted two small yellow stickers on both of the babies' incubators. She asked the nurse on duty that night what they meant, and the nurse replied that in almost thirty years of her being in the hospital she had never seen the likes of what had happened. Kym asked her to explain and was more than delighted to hear that a second set of twins with the same unusual surname as her own had been admitted the same night that Kym had asked for a sign that her babies would be OK. Again, proof that God and the angels will work with you, but remember you have to ask!

In February 2005, Stephen and I were on our way to work and were chatting away as we did to pass the time, when we came upon a notorious junction on the N2. All of a sudden I felt the van swerve to the right. A gentleman in a jeep was trying to cross from one side of the N2 to the other as we were passing the junction. He did not see us approaching and still proceeded to cross. He hit our van with a good bang, which sent us careering across the other side of the road. We then hit the bank and veered out on to the wrong side of the road for a second time. For those few seconds I could neither see nor hear any traffic on this busy road. But upon coming to a stop the traffic, which included forty-foot trucks, reappeared. The emergency services were there very quickly and one of the firemen that was cutting me out of the van said that somebody must have been watching over us that day – when they get a call to that junction it is normally a fatal accident. I recall what was going through my mind at the moment he said those words: I had smiled to myself and knew that it was in fact Archangel Michael who had saved us from serious injury, as I always ask for his protection prior to making any journey.

I have been asked to do many, many readings over the years, and it has been an honour and a pleasure to be able to pass messages of comfort from loved ones. Sometimes I'm asked to do readings away from home.

In 2007 I was asked to do angel readings on a Spirit of the Sea cruise. I agreed, but I was a little worried. I felt this would be out of my comfort zone. We flew to Newcastle to get the ship, which sailed to Amsterdam and back to Newcastle. People were booking readings in advance of the cruise. That worried me too. But Andrew was reassuring.

'It will be OK,' he said.

And it was. Some of the readings were amazing. I was given very strong messages to pass on. The first woman I read for gave me the following testimonial.

From the moment I walked into the room I felt at ease with this beautiful lady. Her whole being exuded love and light and a spirit that shone. With her tiny frame, lovely long dark hair and piercing blue eyes, I felt as though I was meeting someone very special. Patricia is just that. Her precision astounded me, including names and times and events. Her true humility shone from her eyes as she gave me details that could *never* be a second guess or shot in the dark. I could have quite easily spent all day with her, but all too soon our time was over. I left the room feeling elated and more lifted than I had done in a long time. She gave me true evidence of the Angels and Spirit World.

This evidence was also proven later on in the evening. Patricia had given me healing upon my stomach area which she told me had been troubling me (very true!). Later I had an Aura Reading by another lady and the Solar Plexus Chakra (stomach area) showed up as very strong (at 90 per cent balanced!), much stronger than the other chakras. Usually this is the weakest chakra for me. This proves beyond doubt that Patricia, along with the Angels and Spirit World, had performed something that cannot be dismissed. Patricia is a humble, special and very gifted lady. I would recommend her very highly to anyone that is thinking of guidance from the

Angels or communication with a lost loved one. She has undoubtedly got a God-given gift which she shares with those who seek her. She is most certainly an Earth Angel.

There were other healers on the cruise. One was a man called Lawrence Leyton. He had done a programme for Channel 4 on fear of flying. He was giving a show, and I was determined to go and see it, so I made sure I finished the readings on time. I'm so glad I did, because he is amazing. He asked for ten volunteers on the stage.

I've never seen so many people rush up to the stage in all my life. He chose just ten, and he started bringing them back in time. It was as if he was hypnotizing them, but I was impressed with the calm way he was doing it. I've seen hypnotists before – the ones who make people do really silly things on stage – but Lawrence wasn't like that. He was bringing them all back in time. He'd only allow happy memories.

There was one man who seemed to become very deeply hypnotized. Lawrence was bringing him right back in time. He touched the man on the shoulder, and asked him what year he was in. The man said he was in 1900. He gave his name back then, his age, and he explained how many children he had. He then started to say that he felt sick.

Lawrence brought him to the point where, in his previous life, he had just passed over. That was the most amazing thing. People were sitting on the edge of their seats listening to this man. Lawrence without a doubt proved to me that there is a past life. We all have one, we did exist before and we do come back, maybe in a different religion, a different race.

After the performance, Lawrence and I got chatting.

I said to him, 'That was amazing. I couldn't believe what I was seeing.'

'Well, Patricia, that was the first time I've been able to do that on stage. I do bring people back to a past life; that can happen often, but normally I would do that privately.'

Lawrence then asked me to do a reading for him. I did, and he was pleased. Later, I told him that I have a fear of flying. We were interrupted then. A magazine photographer came along, and I forgot all about it. So when we were due to fly back on the Monday I got myself in a bit of a tizzy.

It's strange. I didn't really understand my fear. I'm not scared of dying. How could I be when I know there's an afterlife? But there was something about planes, something that really scared me.

So there we were in the airport. Lawrence and Stephen and some of the others were having breakfast. I couldn't face any. Not with the thought of getting into that aeroplane. Lawrence noticed.

'Are you not going to have something?' he asked. 'Something small, and a drink maybe?'

'Lawrence, I couldn't even think of it.'

'Why?'

'I told you. I'm terrified of flying.'

'Come over here,' he said, 'and sit down beside me.'

I did that, but I was finding it hard to sit still. We'd all been joking, and I told him if he looked in my eyes I was bound to start laughing. That's when Andrew popped up.

'You're really going to have to listen to this man,' he said. I told Andrew to go away. All I could think about was getting back on that plane. Then Lawrence spoke.

'Patricia, imagine your fear,' he said.

And I started laughing again. 'Well, that's difficult.'

'Why?'

'Because I've more than one fear. I'm worried the pilot is

going to faint. I worry an engine is going to stop . . . there are all sorts of fears going on with me.'

'Just imagine it as a stamp.'

I tried to.

'Now your fear is getting smaller.' He tapped me on the knee. That's all he did. Nothing else. I couldn't believe it, but my fear seemed to have gone. A friend, Gerry Vickers, was with us that day. He's a reiki master. He knew I was scared of flying and he couldn't believe it when I was almost first in the queue. There was not a bother out of me.

I got on the plane that day and I was fine. My fear had gone and it's never come back. Not to this day. And I have Lawrence Leyton to thank for that.

I don't give formal readings when we go on holiday, but often when Stephen and myself are away I'm asked to pass on a message. It happened last year, when we went to the Isle of Man. We took a four-day break last June. We went to a castle where they were doing tours. A woman guide directed us on which way to go, but after I had admired the scene in the castle, I found myself going back up the steps to the guide instead of going straight on as she'd told me. I was drawn back to her. The guide was standing at the top of the stairs. She laughed when she saw me.

'Have you made a wrong turn?'

I looked at her and said, 'Do you mind if I say something to you?'

'Oh, you're not one of those mediums, are you?'

I just smiled. 'I don't know about that, but do you mind if I say something?' I could see the spirit world with her.

'Go on, then.'

'Your sister is with you.'

She really looked at me then. 'It's my sister's anniversary today,' she said.

'Well, your sister is happy. It was your brother's fortieth birthday recently.' She nodded. 'And you felt really sad because your sister wasn't there.'

'Yeah. You're right. Oh my God.'

I didn't want to go to the castle that day. But Stephen had said, 'Oh, come on.' That's the spirits' way of saying, 'Please give someone a message.'

It happened again. The night before we came home, we'd been on a horse and trap. The horses all had names on them. We decided to get the trap to a Chinese restaurant down at the end of the pier. We'd have our meal, then walk back. We waited in line for our horse. As it came along, I said to Stephen, 'Look at the name of the horse.'

'Oh my God.' The horse's name was John. I knew John's spirit was there. We went down, had our food and had a slow walk back up the pier. There was a new ship coming in. We stopped to look. The waves were getting stronger, from the wake. We decided to go. It was getting late, half past eleven, and I was getting cold as I had no coat on me. As we were walking off, two ladies and a gentleman stopped and were looking over the wall.

Stephen said, 'We were just admiring that ship there.' He fell into conversation with the man and I was talking to the man's wife and his mother-in-law. They were from Belfast.

I was about to say goodbye when I looked at the gentleman and started to cry. Stephen looked at me, and said, 'Oh no. Here we go again. Are you all right?'

I said, 'No.' I got so emotional. I said to the man, 'Do you mind if I speak to you?'

Stephen explained about the angels, and the man's wife

asked if she could take the message for him. She was mad into readings, but her husband wasn't.

'You can stand with him,' I said, 'but the message is not for you.'

The man had lost his father, and then his sister, in tragic accidents. He had only lost his sister a couple of months previously to us meeting him. He was absolutely heartbroken. So I sat him down and gave him the message: his sister, who had died in a car accident, didn't blame him. He'd felt guilty about his sister's death. He was to have given her a lift that night, but wasn't able to. His sister told me to tell him that it wasn't his fault. She just wasn't watching what she was doing.

It was amazing how we were there at the same time. The man said he'd felt drawn to the Isle of Man, but didn't know why, and I'd had no plans to visit either. I always go where I am drawn to go. I know it's the spirit world bringing me to these places. That's the way the spirit world works with me. If they want to give a message they will, but I won't call them. There are so many stories like that, and often they happen when I've been away.

21 Understanding the Past

The angels talk to me, and tell me where to find
someone who needs me.

My dad is nearly seventy now. Not that he will tell you. Dad has always had a thing about age. All he will say is that he was born in a leap year. Dad is still a charmer. He still looks after himself too. His hair is grey now; not black as it once was. But he still keeps it neatly combed. And he still polishes his shoes. Everything has to be 'just right'. That's the military in him.

Ten years ago my father rang me. He sounded worried.

'Trish, I need to talk to you.'

'I'm listening.'

'No, Trisha. I mean face to face.'

I went to see him, and he said, 'Have you heard the stories about the abuse in the Industrial Schools? Schools like Artane?'

'Yeah. I don't like reading that stuff in the papers, because it's negative. But you can't help being aware of the stories. Those poor boys!'

'Yeah,' he said. 'Yeah. Well, Trish, I was one of them.'

I remember just sitting down and looking at him. I was stunned. There were two angels around him. I remember one angel saying, 'That is why he is the way he is.' And I knew then that was why I could never hate him. All those years when he had put us all through so much, I had sensed that something had made him the man he was.

'Trish, I need your help. I need you to come with me to my counsellor. I can't go if you don't come too.'

I went to every counselling session with him. It was terrible because he had to go through every single detail again and again. I made the train journey with him, and he would be nervous going over. He would pretend it wasn't bothering him, but he'd be tapping his knee. And that's a sign that he's worried.

When he'd had a few sessions, the counsellor decided to hypnotize him, to bring him back to the worst memories. I didn't want to be in the room when that happened, but he said, 'Please don't leave me.' He seemed so vulnerable. I really did not want to be in that room. I couldn't bear the thought of hearing his bad memories.

So I said to the angels, 'Please don't let me hear what he says,' and all I could hear in my ears was singing. Even so, I will never forget that day. I remember just sitting in this big room, and the counsellor was talking him through his memories. I'd never seen my dad cry. Never. But that day his tears were like a river. I couldn't hear, but I could see his physical pain. I felt like I was going through the pain with him.

When he came out of the hypnosis, he sat up and said, 'Why am I crying? Where is this coming from?'

When the stories about Artane came out, my dad had to acknowledge what he put his children through. And he did acknowledge it. He had to. He took a case to the high court. In the end, when they'd bullied him into this, that and the other, they settled it.

The solicitor gave me a copy of my dad's report. It made me so sad to read it. Dad had gone to Artane for mitching.

When the family moved to Ballyfermot, he only went to school two and a half days a week. He started selling newspapers at Heuston Station – or Kingsbridge as it was then – and he worked on a cattle-boat earning half a crown. The first time he went to court for mitching he was let off. The second time he was sent to Artane for three years.

Dad couldn't believe it. He was really angry with my grandfather. When the judge asked him why he didn't make sure Dad went to school, he said he couldn't because he couldn't take the time off work. Dad felt he could have done. When Granddad went to visit Dad in the holding cell, Dad wouldn't even see him. I don't think Dad ever forgave his Granddad.

Artane was just terrible. Dad ate bread and margarine, and the dinners, with cabbage and very little meat, had always gone cold before the boys got to them. The boys got up at five thirty every morning. Then there was a sheet inspection. If the sheets were wet, they were tied around the boy's neck, and the other boys lined up and hit him on the head as they paraded down the dormitory. Dad didn't wet the bed when he first arrived – but he did when the abuse started. He said he was afraid to go to sleep.

One time, Dad tried to run away. He got as far as a cottage just before the main road, and then he was caught. He had to stand, all night, facing the wall. And the next morning he was whipped in front of the whole school. A brother whipped him across his legs and his backside and the backs of his hands. Then his head was shaved and he was sent to Coventry. He was sore for weeks, and badly bullied too.

Dad was beaten every day, and he was abused at least four nights every week. There were two different brothers who abused him. When, after loads of beatings, he couldn't walk and went to the infirmary, he was abused there too. Then he was sent to Cappagh Hospital to help his legs heal. He was tied down in bed and couldn't move. Then, when his legs were better, he had to be taught how to walk again. Dad spent eighteen months in Cappagh Hospital. It can't have been easy, but he was happier there than in Artane, because the nuns were kind. He felt safe there. When he got back to Artane, and learned tailoring as a trade, life was not quite as bad as it had been before. By the time he got home, he'd been away for four and a half years.

Dad talked about his life after Artane for the report too. He talked about his drinking, and about being thrown out of the army. He said he'd lost jobs because of his drinking too. He said when he drank he remembered what had happened in Artane. The bad memories all came back and he couldn't cope with them. That is why he was the way he was.

Dad was on antidepressants for years. He spent time in St Ita's psychiatric hospital. Poor Dad. I realize now, he hadn't a chance.

He said in the report that he beat his children. He said he lost it if we lied, or got too close to the traffic. Reading that made such a difference to me. It made me see him in a whole different light.

Dad always relied on me. All my family did. That could be hard. They thought I was strong. They didn't realize that I was hurting too.

When the counselling and the Artane report were going on, I'd sometimes have a phone call at three o'clock in the morning. It would be Dad. He'd say, 'I can't do this. I can't do it any more.' And I'd hear this train. And I'd have to go searching for him on the train track where he was going to kill himself. He would always ring me. And the angels would talk to me and tell me where to find him. He sees me as being the strong one. That was it. It was, *You can cope*.

I have this barrier I have to keep up. I still have it to this day. It doesn't matter how much I am hurting, or how much pain I am in, I will not give in. I don't want my family to see I am hurting. I want to be strong for them. Everyone says, 'Trish is strong.' They all come to me now.

One good thing, Dad is proud of me. He brags about me now. Because I've done readings for people he knows. He's as proud as punch. He'll say, 'That's my daughter. My eldest daughter.' That makes me feel so good.

It has been a long journey to come to terms with my childhood and one that I continue to take. I am very thankful and grateful to the angels and to my guardian angel, Simone, and, of course, to my wonderful spirit guide, Andrew, without whom I don't know where I would be. It is with their help and guidance that even after everything that happened to me I have a loving relationship with Mam and Dad.

I could never hate Mam because I knew she was suffering too. Mam and I have had long chats since my brother John passed away and we have been very open and honest with each other. One evening I was visiting Mam and Dad and I was telling them about having written this book and they both listened to me with so much pride and love.

Mam said, 'Patricia, did you tell how it really was?'

I asked her what did she mean and she said, 'Did you say how you got slapped around and how you all went hungry?'

I looked at my poor mam's face and my heart sank. She seemed so old. I hadn't noticed it before. I really had to hold back the tears.

I said, 'Yes, Mam, I did.'

Then she said, 'Good, I'm happy now.'

I gave her a hug and she said she was sorry. I told Mam she had no need to say sorry to me. She said, 'Oh, but I do.' She was sorry for not hugging us when we were little, for not telling us she loved us.

I told Mam that didn't matter because we always loved her and Dad. Always and still do.

Now, when I go to visit Mam and Dad it's not sad any more. We all had some sort of healing from the angels and Mam and Dad now talk to the angels and get signs, and they love telling me about it.

Dad is so much more relaxed now. He does all the cooking for Mam. He still likes to have a drink but doesn't get angry. He loves a laugh and a joke now. And he loves winding us up. One day my sister Debbie rang me and asked, 'Do you drink soup or eat it?' I just knew Dad had started this one. My answer was that it depended on whether it was plain soup or a thick vegetable soup.

She had me on loudspeaker and Dad heard my answer and laughed and said, 'I told you, Debs. I'm right 'cause Yaya said what I said.'

He kept that debate going for two days.

What I'm trying to say is Mam and Dad's house is now a happy home. I love them both and I feel so blessed that in spite of everything we still have a bond. Mam and Dad now have sixteen grandchildren and eight great-grandchildren.

22 John

Yaya means 'The Blessed One'.

In January 2009, we were busy preparing for Kym's hen weekend, when I got this sudden urge to ring my brother John, who was living in London.

I told Kym, 'My gut feeling is to ring John. Will you remind me later on?' She said she would.

The next day we were so busy, I forgot. On that Sunday night I had a dream about John. I could see him at the end of my bed. He was standing there looking at me. In the dream I was saying, 'Why are you so calm-looking?'

'Oh, Yaya, I'm here to see you.'

I was telling Kym about my dream when we were on our way to work on Monday, 26 January.

'I have to ring John later on.'

'Mam, why not wait until you get home and have your dinner? You know what it's like when you and John get talking.'

'What's it like?'

She laughed. 'You're on the phone for hours!'

'OK, then.' But all that day my heart was heavy. It was the kind of feeling I would get when I knew something was wrong. When we got home, Dutcho, our little Yorkie, was at the gate as normal to greet us. But she was crying. And at that moment I knew something was wrong. I looked at Kym.

'That's strange,' I said. 'She never cries.'

I went into the house and Stephen was in the kitchen. I knew by the look in his eyes that something was wrong. I looked at Stephen and asked what it was and before he had chance to say anything, I said, 'It's John, isn't it?'

Stephen just looked at me.

'John's dead, isn't he?'

'Yes. I am so sorry, Trish, he is. Mark called about ten minutes ago with the news.'

So John's spirit had come to me that night. He had died on the Sunday in his sleep. And he came to me on the Sunday night to let me know that he had gone.

I had always been extremely close to my brother John. Always. Of all my brothers and sisters, he was the one I had a special bond with. He left home when he was about sixteen. He was a free spirit. He never ever seemed to be able to settle, or to stay in the one place. He liked being outdoors, and was never happier than when he was in the wild.

John had more schooling than I did; he left school when he was fourteen. But he never settled in school. It wasn't that he lacked intelligence. I think school just didn't suit him. He loved animals. He'd rescue them and spend his own money feeding them. He was really, really rock solid.

John was still at home when I married. He was a groomsman at the wedding. I made him wear a suit and he hated that. He wouldn't smile in any of the photos.

I'll never forget when John first went on his travels. He didn't take much. Just a small rucksack and his guitar. I saved up and bought him his first guitar when he was fourteen and a half. He taught himself how to play. He was very musical and he was into art. He could look at a person and within seconds he'd have sketched them. That was his gift.

John was very spiritual. He never said that he could see angels, but he was aware of something, I'm sure of it. He used to talk of 'the higher self'. This was later. Not when we were still children.

John had a difficult childhood. Being the eldest boy wasn't easy. He took the brunt of Dad's temper. Maybe that was why he started drinking so early. He started when he was about thirteen. And this was heavy drinking too. It was certainly why he decided, eventually, to leave Ireland. He felt he had to go away. He always said that he just could not live in Ireland.

Looking at John, you wouldn't think he was a drinker. He didn't have that destructive temperament. He was a peace-maker. If John saw someone arguing, he was quite likely to go over and persuade them to talk it through. John was a really lovely-looking man too. Women loved him. He had a string of girlfriends. He had one in every port, because he was a rambler, but he never married; never had any children. I think that's sad.

When John first left home he went to Cork and worked on a farm. That would be his ideal job because it was outdoors. He got his board and keep, and a bit of payment. After that he came back to Dublin and lived with me for a while. It was when Stephen was a baby. He stayed for about a year, and left just after Alan was born. That time he'd dyed his hair blond. He was in a David Bowie mode, but I really didn't like it. His girlfriend then was called Paula.

I loved having John there. I loved his manner, his gentle-ness. He used to write these songs. He lived with Stephen and myself several times, and I learned to tell when he was about to leave. He would come into the sitting room with his guitar, and write a song. Stephen would say, 'Don't have her in tears now. She's not going to want you to go.'

He would play the song he had written then he'd put the guitar on his back, and say, 'I really do have to go now.'

And off he'd go. I wouldn't see him for maybe a couple of months, but he always wrote to me. He would let me know that he was OK. I was his link with the family. We always kept in touch; there was never a time when we didn't.

When he was living with me and Stephen he hadn't a job. But he'd go off looking for work, and get a day here and a day there. He'd work in a garage maybe. I remember one time, I was telling him not to drink too much. I said, 'Just have a couple of cans, maybe, at night.'

But he had a brainwave. While we were at work, he thought he'd go and buy himself some cans. But he hadn't a car, and our house is miles from the shop. That didn't stop him. He took our horse and jockeyed it bareback to the pub, tied it outside, bought his cans and jockeyed it back up. He hoped we'd never know, but of course we were told. Everyone who saw him thought it was hilarious.

John was in Scotland for a few years. He met a girl there and she moved with him to Birmingham. I really thought these two were going to get married, but John had said, 'I'm not marrying her.'

She didn't like John's drinking. She drank, but not as much as him. It ended up that they got two separate flats right next door to each other. She would come in and tidy up, and he made her meals. That was the way it was with the two of them. They were so funny together, and those two went on like this for ten years.

In between, John came back to Ireland. He lived in Wicklow somewhere. And there were times he'd come back to me. Sometimes with his girlfriend, and sometimes by himself. Stephen was happy about that. He has no brothers, and he always got on well with John; he was like a big brother to him.

John and his girlfriend ended up in London. But then she went back to Scotland because her mam became ill, and then she decided she wasn't coming back any more. John said he was happy, because he wasn't going to have to listen to her ear-bashing, as he called it.

His alcohol dependency started getting very, very strong. John did try to stop. He really did. He went in and out of rehab centres, and he'd do really well while he was there. But when he came out, and there was no backup, he'd slip back again.

One time, while he was in there, he started studying. He was fascinated by the holy shroud. He loved history. It was after that he got his little flat in London. He was in that flat for eight or nine years before he died.

He came over to Ireland about twice a year. And in between we just knew how each other was. We always knew. We knew when something was wrong with each other, even though he was there and I was here.

The last time I saw him, I knew something was wrong with him. It wasn't that he looked especially sick. He looked pretty much himself. He went back to London and soon after I rang to tell him that Kym had decided she was getting married. He was over the moon.

'I hope my invite is in the post.'

'Of course,' I said. 'You are top of the list.'

I worried about him then, because his voice didn't sound right. Not to me. So I asked him straight out, 'Are you OK, John?'

'Yeah, yeah. I'm fine,' he said.

That didn't reassure me, because I knew John too well. And he'd never tell me, even if he was ill.

He came over at the start of December 2008. He went to stay with Mam and he was there for almost a week. I didn't even know he'd been over. That was so out of character. At the time Mam was really surprised.

'Why are you not at Patricia's house?' she said. That's when he told her. Told her the terrible news.

'I'm sick, Mam. I'm sick, and I don't want Patricia to know.'

'Why would she know? I couldn't tell, if you hadn't told me.'

'Ah, but Patricia would. You know her! One look into my eyes and she'd know for sure.' Then he told Mam that his liver was bad and that he hadn't long to live. He was only forty-three. She didn't tell us. He said to her, 'I can't face telling Patricia.'

'You're going to have to tell her.'

'No. I don't want to.'

'But that will hurt her.'

'Not if I leave a message with you. Will you please let Patricia know that I have always loved her, and I've always known that she loved me. And tell her that she wasn't only my sister – she was my mam.' He'd tell everyone he had two mams – Mam and me.

'Please tell her that yourself.'

'I can't. I can't say goodbye to her. It would hurt us both so much.'

There was no insurance for him, and Mam and Dad wanted him brought home from London. Myself and Stephen flew out to London on the Thursday after he died. This was the time of the bad snow, so it wasn't the easiest of journeys. I arrived in London on the Thursday, and the snow was bad in London too. I was supposed to make it to the death registry office on the Friday, but there were no staff there – they hadn't been able to get in because of the snow.

We ended up waiting until the Monday. But, anyway, the flights had been cancelled because of the snow. I registered him on the Monday, but then I had to find a funeral home. I approached several and they said they could bring John home to Ireland for us, but it was going to cost £20,000. Without insurance, there was no way I could pay that kind of money. I thought, *Oh, angels, what am I going to do?*

They said, 'It won't cost you £20,000. Don't worry about it!'

And they were right. We came across a place called Kenyan Funeral Home in Notting Hill, and they were excellent. Their charge was £1,800 and I could afford that. Just.

When John's body arrived at the funeral home, they rang us and asked if we could bring some clothes up for him. I'd already been down to his flat, and had picked up his leather jacket. He loved that so much. I hardly ever saw him out of it! I found his wallet there. There wasn't a lot of money in it, but I found his miraculous medal on its blue ribbon. That made me smile. I'd given him that medal when he was thirteen, and I'd told him to be careful and always have it with him. There was a photograph of me too. And there was a condom. And that made me smile even more.

When John was twelve years old, I was trying to clean the house. As I was washing the kitchen floor, John kept coming in and out and in and out. He said, 'Why do you call me John, when everyone else calls me Johnny?'

He kept asking, and then he mentioned a condom. 'Everyone calls a condom a johnny, so I must be a condom.'

I'd giggled then.

'No, you're not!'

'Well, what is a condom?'

'You can ask me that when you're my age.'

When he was seventeen, he was visiting me, and he said, 'Look.' He pulled a condom out of his pocket. 'I'm going to always carry one of these in my pocket, and it will always make me think of when I asked you that question.'

While I was looking at that, my sister Liz, who lives in London, picked up the rest of his clothes, and said she'd meet us at the funeral parlour.

We went down and went in. There was an attractive girl in there, dealing with us. She was young and had a lovely manner. Her name was Alexandra.

'I'm just waiting for my sister to come with his jeans,' I told her.

'That's fine,' she said. 'Go and get yourself a sandwich and a cup of tea while you're waiting. There's a good café just across the road.'

We found it, and were chatting over our tea when Alexandra rang us.

'Patricia, your sister hasn't turned up. We really need John's clothes within the next hour. It's important. I know you want an open coffin when you get him home.' I rang my sister, who said she was on her way, so I decided the safest thing was to go and buy John some new clothes.

Myself and Stephen were in Notting Hill. It's a nice enough place, but we'd never been there before. We didn't know where to go to find a clothes shop, and the pavements were compacted with hard snow. We were slip-sliding everywhere. There were some lovely shops in Notting Hill. Lovely food shops and bookshops, but we couldn't see a men's clothes shop.

When we left the funeral home we turned right, not knowing where we were going. After a couple of yards we stood in the middle of the path trying to figure out which way we should go. We met a gentleman from the funeral home who had nipped out for a quick smoke. We asked him where to go to get clothes for John. He said if we wanted a suit to carry on into the more upmarket area. We both laughed together and said no, that just a pair of jeans and a jumper would do. John would not have thanked us if we had put a suit on him. Anyway, he told us the best place was to go down to Portobello which was about five minutes in the other direction. It took us about half an hour to get there with the amount of snow and ice on the paths and roads. We passed so many clothes shops, but they were all for ladies. All of them. We kept walking, and there was not one men's shop in sight. We were making such slow progress in the snow, because we had to hang on to one another so that we wouldn't fall flat on our faces. We were giggling. That felt wrong, when John had died, but we could see the humour of it all. At the same time, underneath, I was starting to panic.

We got to Portobello Road and we could either turn left and have to go uphill or turn right to go down. We chose right as it would be easier to slide down than try to make our way up. We walked for about ten minutes and could not find a men's clothes shop. We could see a bridge in the distance.

'Let's just go as far as that bridge,' said Stephen, pointing down the road. 'Let's see what happens then.'

We got to the bridge and it was still all women's clothes. We asked an old man with a walking stick, who was making his way, slowly, along the pavement.

'Just keep walking down,' he said. 'And you'll come to one.'

I started joking then. 'John, I'm sorry, but you're going to get buried in a dress at this rate.'

I stopped then, and tried to connect with John. 'John, we need a men's shop. If we don't find one soon, you're going home in the same state you were born. You'll travel with nothing on you.'

The next minute, Stephen said to me, 'Trish. Look across the road.'

'What?'

'Look.' He pointed. 'Over there.'

I turned and looked. And there was a men's shop. A shop called Yaya of London. I thought, *Yaya? Oh my God!* It took us a while to cross the road. The traffic was really heavy, but we went in and saw two African men serving. One of them reminded me of my spirit guide, Andrew. So much so that when I looked at him I just said, 'Oh,' out loud.

He came over and said, 'Can I help you?'

Stephen explained that John had died, and that we needed to get him some jeans.

'It has to be jeans,' he explained. 'Because that's all he used to wear.'

The assistant found some jeans, but they were designer ones, and had a price to match. And I knew John would hate me buying those. He lived a very simple life.

I said to the assistant, 'It's not that I don't want to spend that amount of money on my brother, it just wouldn't be right. He wouldn't like it.'

He looked at me as if I was mad. He just didn't understand. I explained again.

'How tall was your brother?' he said.

It suddenly hit me then, what we were actually doing. I couldn't discuss it any more. So I walked out of the shop. Stephen went on talking, and when I got back, Stephen had picked out some jeans. He'd picked a navy jumper too, with a zip up the front.

'I'm so sorry about your brother,' the man said. And I could see he genuinely was sorry. I was feeling better again, and I got curious.

'Where did the name for your shop come from?' I asked. 'Why is it called Yaya?'

'Why do you want to know?' He looked defensive. I think he thought I was slagging him.

'It's just, my family call me Yaya. They've called me that for years.'

'Well, it actually comes from the Bible, from John the Baptist.'

'But what does it mean?'

'It means "The Beloved One".'

I got really emotional then. I thought, *How nice is that? That name was given me by Mark, and that's what it means.* As we were leaving the gentleman gestured to us to take a T-shirt as a gift for my brother. Printed on the T-shirt was their logo, 'Yaya of London'.

We said goodbye to the man, and started walking up the hill. And I don't know if you've tried to walk uphill on compacted ice, but it's not easy. We were walking up, and I was just thanking the angels. Then, suddenly, I could hear John's voice. He said, 'I'm not going without socks.'

'What?'

'You didn't get me socks.'

I got into a real panic then. I stopped dead, and Stephen, who was still hanging on to me, almost fell over.

'What's the matter, Trish?'

'Oh, Stephen, socks! I never got socks.'

John had this thing that he didn't like his feet being bare.

'Don't panic. Don't panic. Look, there's a stall over there.'

And there was. There was a stall selling all kinds of bits and pieces, scarves, and hats. 'Stay here,' said Stephen and he rushed over to the stall. I could see him pick up a bundle of something and hand over a coin, and when he came back, sure enough, he had five pairs of white socks.

'And only two pounds,' he said, with a grin. We were some way away from the stall at that stage. Suddenly we heard this almighty crash. We both looked around. It was like someone had kicked the stall. There was stuff rolling around everywhere. The man was standing there scratching his head, as if to say, 'How did that happen?'

'I hope nothing is broken,' I said. And Stephen reassured me, saying there was nothing breakable on the stall. But I felt responsible. It reminded me of a scene in the movie *Ghost*. I had the feeling that John's spirit was following us. I was sure of it. And I think kicking over the stall was his way of making us notice him. I think it was his way of saying, 'Thanks.'

We went back up, and gave the clothes in. John was to fly out the following Thursday on the flight behind us. We flew, but his flight was cancelled. Now, John hated flying. He tried it once and hated it so much that I could never get him on a plane again. He always travelled by boat after that. Could he have been trying to get out of flying, even now he was dead?

If so, it didn't work. His plane flew in on the Friday. There was just one thing. It had to go to Belfast first. Now, John loved Belfast. I think he felt, if he had to fly, he might as well see Belfast one more time.

I was in Mam and Dad's house when John arrived. I went into the kitchen and said, 'John's home now.'

I expected them to rush to the coffin, but they just looked

at each other and didn't move. They just couldn't do it. Stephen and I were the ones to bring him into the sitting room. When the lid was taken off, I fixed him up. He had a shroud around him, and I felt he wouldn't want that. I felt he'd want to be free. I fixed his hands and his hair. While I was doing that I said, 'At last I can mess with your hair, and you can't have a go at me.'

John loved his hair. He'd change the style often. Sometimes it was long, sometimes short, and sometimes he dyed it blond. When he died, it was brown with a reddish hue. That was his natural colour. He always had loads of freckles. He never lost those.

Mam had John waked in the house from the Friday until the Sunday. He was cremated on the Tuesday, and his coffin was open, in the sitting room, in the meantime. The thing was, though, that nobody would go into that room if I wasn't there. Not one of them. They all found being there with him really difficult. It was like they relied on me to be there.

I didn't resent that. Not at all. But I did feel that I couldn't grieve properly. I had to be strong. To be strong for them.

It was terrible losing John when he was just forty-three. I miss him so much. But I can't be too sad. I do still see John a lot. He was always smiling when he was alive. And now, in heaven, he has this beam of light which is constantly around him. I see him, and I hear him. I know he's happy in heaven. Happier there than when he was here. His spirit is free.

John is still so close to me. He reminds me, every day, that spirits in heaven are happy. When he was alive John was always searching for something. But he didn't know what he was searching for.

On his first anniversary, January 2010, I set off a lantern

with a message. As it was going into the sky, I heard John say, 'I've found my purpose.'

He always reckoned he was only put on earth for a short time. And that heaven is where he belongs. He is doing good work in heaven. He looks after the souls of people who have committed suicide. He is a guiding light to them.

It's John who is responsible for this book. He said it to me, when he died.

'It's time,' he said. 'Now is the time, Patricia, for you to write your book.'

'Are you sure?'

'Write it, Patricia. Do that, and it will end a lot of pain and suffering for a lot of people. For people outside the family and in.'

Tall Candle

Tall candle oh so bright,
Always there to give us light,
Guide our way on cold dark nights,
Take away our fear and frights.
In the day you hide away,
But come night's fall you're out to play,
To cast your light upon each wall,
Making shadows small and tall.
Designs of your one will make
In your marvellous waxing lake.
But now my eyes feel strained with light,
So tall candle I bid you goodnight.

*(Written by John when he was thirteen,
and read out at his funeral)*

Epilogue

I believe everybody is born with the ability to communicate with angels. Many children have imaginary friends. I believe the imaginary friends are really angels. But when children go to school and go out with their friends, they don't want to talk to angels any more. And as life gets busy it can make us forget them.

I think the angels stayed with me because I didn't have other close friends, and because I needed them to help me with my pain. It wasn't that I didn't feel the pain; but they protected me. They told me I was going to have a hard life.

Even now, I know something is going to happen before it happens. The angels give me that pre-warning. They give me that warning to try and ease my pain. I feel other people's pain as well. If I'm with somebody and they are suffering, I feel it and I get very emotional. I'm so sensitive to the energies that are out there.

Communicating with spirits can be very tiring. The angels know that, and my spirit guide, Andrew, is good to me now. If the spirit world is there, and they really do need to speak to me, even if I'm asleep, Andrew has to poke me to make sure I am awake. But the angels know I need a top-up. It's like getting credit on a call card or a charge for your mobile phone.

I get energy by taking time out to be by myself. I won't read. I won't do anything. I'll listen to whatever music I'm in the mood for that day. That music will give me a charge.

Sometimes I go and get an aromatherapy massage. It's about taking care of yourself, because when you take care of yourself, your soul is taken care of too.

My grandchildren Rebecca and Holly talk to angels. They have the confidence to do that. I am so pleased about it. I know Rebecca and Holly are never going to be told to be quiet, because there is a deeper understanding about angels now. Holly's mam is very spiritual, and Rebecca's dad, my older boy, is too. So I know, in those households, those little girls will be allowed to talk to angels and speak about the spirit world. And then, I am here. They can talk to me. They are used to it.

If your child speaks about imaginary friends, or an angel, or someone who has passed on who, maybe, they have never met, believe them. Accept it. But don't make a big thing about it. Never *make* them speak to the spirit world. That's not good either. They will do it in their own time. Just believe the child. Accept what they are saying, and explain to them who the person was.

My granddaughter Rebecca is in school now. She was a bit nervous out in the playground. Last year she said to me, 'What do you do when other children are bold?'

Rather than going back to her with a negative, I said, 'You know the way you talk to the angels and the angels talk to you?'

'Yeah. That's what I want to know, Nanny. Which angel?'

'Call Archangel Michael. And just say to him, "Please can I have your blue coat?" You will see it's really soft.'

'Then what do I do?'

'You put on the pretend coat. Then you ask Archangel Michael to mind you.'

A couple of days later she was up with me. She said, 'Nanny.'

'Yes.'

'That blue coat is great.'

'See!'

'No, really. Because there's a girl in the yard and I saw her coming over to me. She is a bit bold.'

'Is she?'

'Yes. She's a bit older than me. I saw her coming, I shut my eyes and I just went, "Blue coat, please."'

'And what happened then?'

'The girl walked away from me.'

It's wonderful for children. She didn't have to even say the whole sentence. It was, 'Blue coat, please,' and he was there.

Rebecca speaks to her angels every day. She is nine this year and she sees angels. She doesn't go on about it. She has her childhood. If she sees an angel she will tell you. She sees my angel, her mam's angel, her dad's angel.

Whereas Holly, my other granddaughter, is five and she sees the spirit world. One time her mam, Janice, was strapping her into her seat in the car, and as she was leaning across, she noticed Holly waving. Janice turned and looked. She said, 'Holly, who are you waving at?'

'The little girl.'

'But there's nobody there.'

'No, Mam, there she is. She's in my bedroom.'

Janice looked up and said, 'Holly, there is nobody there.'

Holly said, 'But, Mammy, she *is* there.'

'Well, who is it, then?'

'It's Chloe. My little sister, Chloe.'

Now, Holly didn't know her mother had lost a baby. Janice always had a feeling it was a little girl, and that was the name she would have called her – Chloe – but the name was never mentioned. Holly was only two and a half when she started seeing her sister.

One time her dad said to her, 'Are you OK, baby?'

'Yeah, I'm grand. I'm playing with my little sister.'

'And what's her name?'

'Chloe.'

So Holly is quite comfortable seeing the spirit world. If somebody dies, she will say, 'Don't worry about them, because they are happy, you know.'

Appendix: How to Communicate with the Angels

The Angels

Archangel Michael is the strongest of the archangels. He is the protector. Sometimes I see him with a sword. He helps to give us strength and courage. We should ask him for help where there is conflict or arguments. Ask Archangel Michael to help when you or any of your family are travelling. Ask him to place a protective ball of white light around you and your family.

Archangel Michael has many angels. These angels make his army of protectors. Each night I ask Archangel Michael to send four of his protectors to stand watch over my home and the homes of my family. I ask that they will guard and protect us through the night and keep us safe and free from all harm.

Archangel Raphael is the healing angel. He has beautiful flowing wings, and a shimmering emerald green light around him. You can ask Archangel Raphael to help with healing on any level. It can be emotional, physical or spiritual healing. Should you need to call upon Archangel Raphael to send healing to a loved one or a friend, ask him to place his green healing balm around the person that needs healing. Know that Archangel Raphael will always be there for you. He is a very gentle but powerful angel.

Archangel Gabriel is good for communication. Ask him for help if you have a job interview, or if you need help with arts and crafts. Archangel Gabriel is the angel who is most called upon by writers and has helped me write this book. He is the angel I give many thanks to.

Archangel Uriel is for inner peace. He's wonderful at giving solace when someone has passed away. He comes in to give inner peace and he helps us to love ourselves again, and not to blame ourselves for things that were beyond our control.

How to Build an Angel Altar

You can build an angel altar anywhere you wish; the size of the altar is immaterial, it can be as simple as a candle and a statue. It really does not matter. Put what you feel is right on your altar.

On my altar I have an angel figurine, a piece of rose quartz stone (which is for love and healing, and also helps aid people in grief), a deck of angel cards, and a white tea-light candle.

I also have a small angel box in which I place my worries. You can use any sort of box for this – it does not have to be an angel box. Write down your worries and place them in your box, and then ask the angels to help you.

If someone you know is sick, write down their name on a piece of paper, place it in the box, and ask Archangel Raphael to send some healing to that person. Then place the box on your altar. Always give thanks to the angels.

Your Guardian Angel

Your guardian angel is always with you – since the moment you were conceived, until it is your time to leave this life and go on to the next one.

Your angel waits by your side. You can ask your angel anything you wish. When you ask for help, it doesn't matter how big or small your request is, your angel will always try to help. Remember that your angel is always by your side.

Your angel will help you, or anybody that you request help for. Your angel always knows best. Your angel will be only too happy to help you, but you must remember to always *ask* for your angel's help. We are all born with a free will, and your angel will always respect this free will. That is why you always have to ask for their help.

You may not get the help you asked for straight away, but be assured that your angel *is* helping you, and will help as fast as they can.

If you are worried about a family member, or there has been conflict between two or more people, ask your angel to have a word with their angels. I have found in the past that when you ask for help in this type of situation it really does work.

Always trust your angel. Speak to your angel on a regular basis. The more you talk with your angel, the more connected you will become with them. In time you will find yourself becoming more relaxed.

Speak with your angel just as if you are speaking to a best friend or a loved one. Do not be afraid to have a long chat with them as they are great listeners. They will soon become your best friend, and remember, your angel will always be by your side.

How to Find Out Your Guardian Angel's Name

Ask your angel what their name is. The first name that comes to your head will be your angel's name. To confirm this, you can ask your angel for a sign. You might pick up a book or a paper, and the name you heard will just jump out at you. Or your angel will give a soft breeze across your cheek. Then you know they are with you.

How to Talk to Your Guardian Angel

When I light the candle on my altar I always say, 'I welcome the angels of light into my home.' Then I just talk to Simone.

To get a sense of your angel, just take a few minutes to relax and clear your mind. Ask your angel to let you know if they are around.

That can be hard. You might be thinking, *I have to get the dinner on*, or *I have to put the washing out*. If that thought comes into your mind, just acknowledge it. Acknowledge every thought.

Say, 'OK, I'll put the washing on when I've finished this.' Then the thought goes out of your mind.

Play some gentle music, if you like, then close your eyes. Ask your angel for a sign that they are there with you, and they will give you one. It might be a gentle breeze across your cheek, or a very gentle tug on your hair. Or there might be a very sweet smell, like a spray of roses coming into the room. There may be white feathers. They will give you that sign. Then ask them for help with anything, big or small.

Angels won't give you negative news. They try and guide you onto the right path. They help you to make the right decisions, for your highest good.

To Feel Settled

Archangel Michael taught me a simple technique to make me feel grounded. I put my feet on the ground, and imagine roots going down into the ground. I imagine the roots coming out through the soles of my feet, and they spread out. They slowly come up, and these little branches wrap themselves around my ankles. And then you feel this tug. That always works for me.

To Feel Centred

Imagine a bright light coming through the top of your head, through your body down into the ground, and you are centred.

To Feel Secure

If everything feels too much, or if you feel too buzzy, picture an egg. Close your eyes and imagine this egg, and it's really bright and white. Imagine there's a zip in the egg. You can go into the egg, and you can zip yourself into it. When you are in there, you are protected. The egg is like a shield, and nothing and nobody can harm you while you are in there.

I do that every morning. I create that protection around all my family religiously, every morning. Or I ask Archangel Michael for his ball of white light.

For Children to Feel Secure

Tell children to ask the Archangel Michael for a soft blue coat. Tell them to put this coat on whenever they feel threatened.

Prayer for Healing

This prayer came to me one night:

May Archangel Raphael's healing light
Be in you and around you,

And with his gentle wings to comfort you
As he wraps his wings around you,
Release your pain to him.
Feel his warmth and tender care,
Feel his wondrous green light
That takes away your pain,
Whether it be physical or emotional.

Never give up hope; no matter what is going on in your life. Always remember the angels are by your side, waiting for you to ask for help. Ask your guardian angel for help, and he or she will happily give it to you. Help may not come straight away. But trust and know that your angel will be working hard to help you.

Acknowledgements

I am eternally thankful every day to the angels, to my guardian angel, Simone, and to my wonderful spirit guide, Andrew. Without them I would be lost, as they are a constant strength to me.

Thank you to Patricia Scanlan, who gave me so much encouragement to write this book. There were times that I felt I would never get it finished, but Patricia gave me the kick I sometimes needed; she truly is an earth angel.

A big thank you to Patricia Deevy and all the team at Penguin, who have been there for me. Thanks also to Sue Leonard for all her help in bringing the book together.

Thank you to Julie and Paddy Markey, who made sure I had plenty of soup and sandwiches all the while I wrote this book. Julie and Paddy are like my second mam and dad.

Thank you to Ashlyn Donato from Euro for the supply of pens which were used to write this book.

A big thank you to Mary K Hayden – her friendship means so much. Also a big thank you to Vinnie Woods and Gerry Vickers for the laughter and tears. Warmest thanks to the Cash family too for their support. Huge thanks also for their encouragement and support to Colm and Una Keane, Darren Kinsella, Frank Bambrick of the Local News, Michael and Agnes Fox and Seán and Sarah Russell.

Thank you to all the lovely customers of Angels of Ireland that I have met over the years since we opened.

I cannot thank my family enough, firstly my husband,

Stephen, for all his love and support over the past thirty-one years. Without him I could not have written this book.

To my children, Stephen, Alan and Kym, and their partners, Elaine, Janice and Larry, and love and hugs to my four grandchildren, Rebecca, Holly, Freya and Sean, who mean the world to me.

May the angels bless and watch over every one of you.